ENDC

Sandra Drake has, indeed, learned how to turn her unexpected interruptions into Precious Moments of Intercession. She practices what she preaches!'

Mrs. Anne Spence,
Former Evangel University Prayer Leader
and Wife of Chancellor/Former President
Robert E. Spence

'Sandra Drake's life journey came clearly into focus as a young college student when she wrote the poem, "Traveling on My Knees." It expresses the dynamic of her very successful ministerial and professional life. Managing Interruptions with Moments of Intercession defines the practical, daily application of an intercessory heart to the distractions and interruptions that so often challenge a responsible leader.

Sandra has managed such interruptions throughout an extremely successful missionary and administrative career. As a missionary she served West and East Africa under very stressful circumstances. Later she served as the national director of women's ministries for her church organization. This was followed by becoming the founding director of the National Prayer Center. Her outstanding abilities placed her into constant demand with multiple distractions. We will all do very well to hear her on this subject, for she lives what she has written.'

Dr. Delmer R. Guynes, EDD
President Emeritus, Southwestern Assemblies
of God University

MANAGING INTERRUPTIONS

with

Moments

of

Intercession

Sandra Goodwin Clopine Drake

Scripture taken from the New King James Version. Copyright © 1979, 1980, 1982 by Thomas Nelson, Inc. Used by permission. All rights reserved.

This book is a work of non-fiction. Unless otherwise noted, the author and the publisher make no explicit guarantees as to the accuracy of the information contained in this book and in some cases, names of people and places have been altered to protect their privacy.

LifeRich Publishing is a registered trademark of The Reader's Digest Association, Inc.

LifeRich Publishing books may be ordered through booksellers or by contacting:

LifeRich Publishing
1663 Liberty Drive
Bloomington, IN 47403
www.liferichpublishing.com
1 (888) 238-8637

Because of the dynamic nature of the Internet, any web addresses or links contained in this book may have changed since publication and may no longer be valid. The views expressed in this work are solely those of the author and do not necessarily reflect the views of the publisher, and the publisher hereby disclaims any responsibility for them.

Any people depicted in stock imagery provided by Thinkstock are models, and such images are being used for illustrative purposes only. Certain stock imagery © Thinkstock.

ISBN: 978-1-4897-1003-1 (sc)
ISBN: 978-1-4897-1004-8 (hc)
ISBN: 978-1-4897-1002-4 (e)

Library of Congress Control Number: 2016917049

Print information available on the last page.

LifeRich Publishing rev. date: 11/18/2016

CONTENTS

TRAVELING ON MY KNEES

Last night I took a journey
to a land far 'cross the seas;

I didn't go by boat or plane;
I traveled on my knees.

I saw so many people there
in deepest depths of sin,

And Jesus told me I should go,
that there were souls to win.

But I said, "Jesus, I can't go
and work with such as these."

He answered quickly, "Yes, you can
by traveling on your knees."

He said, "You pray, I'll meet the need;
you call, and I will hear.

Be concerned about lost souls,
of those both far and near."

And so I tried it; knelt in prayer,
gave up some hours of ease.

I felt the Lord right by my side
while traveling on my knees.

As I prayed on, I saw souls saved
and twisted bodies healed,

And saw God's workers' strength renewed
while laboring on the field.

I said, "Yes, Lord, I have a job,
my desire Thy will to please;

I can go and heed Thy call
by traveling on my knees.

—Written by Sandra L. Goodwin in 1957

A SAMPLE PRAYER OF COMMITMENT

Father, I give my moments to You in the interest of others. Regardless of the inconvenience, help me to do my part to bring to You those whose names or faces Your Spirit brings to me.

I give You permission to tear down any walls I have built to protect myself from the world around me. Flood my heart with Your compassion and make me sensitive to those hurting and in need of Your salvation. Give me the ability to be a prayerful intercessor and to see as You see, being less critical and judgmental.

Lord, help me to be Your obedient disciple. At each moment, instill in me an urgency to be available to You that I might do my part in fulfilling the Great Commission.

Thank you for hearing this prayer as I experience the journey of a lifetime, employing my moments in praying for others. In the name of Jesus Christ, my Lord and Savior, I pray. Amen.

_____

(Signature)

_____

(Date)

DEDICATED TO

All those traveling on the journey of life
who encounter interruptions
of one kind or another along the way.

Be encouraged to keep your focus on the God you serve
and His power to prevail, rather than on
the interruptions you encounter and the trauma they create.
You do this by interceding moment by moment
for those around you
who are in great need of God and of
your compassionate care.
You involve yourself with trying to feel what they feel,
so the stings of your own circumstances lessen
as you begin to regain the control which you had lost.
"As you look around right now,
wouldn't you say that in about four
months it will be time to harvest?
Well, I'm telling you to open your eyes
and take a good look at what's right in front of you.
These . . . fields are ripe. It's harvest time"
(John 4:35, The Message).

Now is the time, this is the place, you are the person!

ACKNOWLEDGEMENTS

A number of people have assisted me throughout the years in my preparation for writing this book. There were times when I needed prompting and motivation to continue the process of getting this book re-written and published. My husband, David Drake, has been a very consistent source of encouragement and help in so many ways. He has been readily available to proofread, scan grammatical constructions, and generally assist in any way possible. My love, thanks, and appreciation go to him.

My appreciation and gratitude also go to the Goodwin and Clopine families for the years we traveled together. We went through some tough times, but God saw us through and kept us in His divine care. Many encouraging remarks kept me moving in the direction of producing this book. I will always love and thank God for the times of companionship we had with the knowledge that our God was giving good direction.

The Drake family has filled a very special place in my heart in recent years. They too have helped me focus on this material, and I am grateful for the relationships and contacts we have with each other. All these experiences have contributed to my life story for which I am grateful.

My special gratitude goes to Beverly Graham who has worked diligently on the formatting and preparing of this material for publication. Beverly has had much experience in editing and preparing manuscripts such as this one. I could not have made it through the process without her timely assistance.

LifeRich Publishing has been extremely helpful to me these past months. I so appreciate Doug Horton and Jennifer

Morris for their very capable assistance. Teamwork has been so important in producing this book.

Of course, surrounding it all has been the guidance and help of the Holy Spirit as we have depended upon God at each turn of the road. The admonitions from His Word have moved us to keep a godly perspective: "If my people, which are called by my name, will humble themselves, and pray, and seek my face, and turn from their wicked ways; then I will hear from heaven, and will forgive their sin, and will heal their land. Now My eyes will be open, and My ears attentive to prayer *made* in this place" (2 Chronicles 7:14-15 NKJV).

To God be all the glory!

—Sandra Goodwin Clopine Drake, Author

AUTHOR'S PROLOGUE

Moments of Intercession was published in 1999 by Gospel Publishing House, Springfield, Missouri. At the time I had just retired as director of a National Prayer Center, a position in which I felt I had been sovereignly placed. The experience was a highlight of my life, as were previous positions of leadership in Women's Ministries on both a district and national level. God has led me in awesome ways, and to Him goes all the glory.

Looking back over the circumstances from which I wrote the book, I realize that through the years I have encountered a number of interruptions: those things which break the continuity or uniformity of our lives. As I have read authors speaking to this subject, I have found them to emphasize that we manage interruptions by maintaining focus; keeping control of our time. This line of thought set bells ringing in my head.

"Of course!" Through moments of prayerful intercession, God helped me manage the interruptions in my life. Stepping into the shoes of others and looking at life from their perspective was therapeutic to me during those times when I dealt with my own set of circumstances from day to day. Somehow life became more manageable as I thought on, focused on, and controlled my time with what other people needed and how I could center prayer on them rather than centering on myself.

This must have been the heart of Jesus in Matthew 20:28, *"The Son of Man did not come to be served, but to serve, and to give his life."*

Our humanly mundane circumstances cannot compare to those of our Lord as He set upon the course of giving His life as a ransom for ours. But His commitment to giving could and should become contagious to us who follow Him.

Thus, as I sat down to update this book, I chose to title it *Managing Interruptions with Moments of Intercession.* Also, I felt to include more instances from my life story. As I have walked through life's interruptions in childhood, in ministry, in family relationships, and in my own physical well-being, I have thanked God for burdens He brought to my heart in the interest of others. These were lifelines which I really didn't recognize at the time.

I will share more of that throughout the book, but right now I would like you to read the introduction that you might be blessed in the midst of your own interruptions incorporating moments of intercession on the daily path you walk.

—Sandra G. C. Drake

INTRODUCTION

Prayer moves people in powerful ways. Having served on the Denominational Prayer Leaders Network and the National Association of Evangelicals Board of Directors, I have met with church leaders representing many different denominations. Many of them speak of their congregations finding a refreshing reemphasis on the ministry of prayer. Folks of all backgrounds, all walks of life, and all geographical locations are enjoying renewed fulfillment and joy in spending time with God. Prayer no longer is something to do when all else fails. Prayer involves delighting in a vital, personal relationship with our Lord.

Out of this phenomenal prayer movement have emerged those who feel a special call to the ministry of intercessory prayer. As intercessors, they speak of casting down strongholds, combating spiritual darkness, and praying intensely for long periods of time. Thank God for the burden of prayer they carry and for commitment to His service. We need such people for the times in which we live.

But something has caught my attention. Because of certain terminology, those who do not consider themselves intercessors seem to feel like less important members of the body of Christ. My concern is that no one feel excluded from what God is doing throughout the world today. He is calling us to intercede in prayer for others, whether or not we are known by the term *intercessors.*

In visiting with some who consider themselves ordinary people in the pew, the concept of intercessory prayer virtually overwhelms them. My dad was one of those. He compared himself with people who felt a special calling to intercession, as my mother did, and felt he came up short in God's eyes.

People like my dad might hesitate to believe that Jeremiah 33:3 is for them: *"Call to Me, and I will answer you, and show you great and mighty things, which you do not know."* Intimidated by their seemingly insignificant time in prayer compared to that of prayer warriors who pray more intently, some have become apathetic about praying at all. At a women's retreat, I heard a young Christian mother ask, "What good are my prayers compared to those of real intercessors? I want to be an intercessor, but I'm just an ordinary church member."

The truth is that every Christian has a place in this ministry. Intercessory prayer is a gift God has bestowed upon His Church. It is also our gift to others, energizing our love and service to them. We can open our hearts to the world around us in a moment of time, making ourselves available to the Holy Spirit.

As He impresses us to pray for someone's need, mountains of pain or opposition can be removed. Intercessory prayer can be long and intense, or it can be a powerful moment of intimate, focused faith in God.

My prayer is that the message of this book will serve as a helpful tool for all who desire to intercede moment by moment. This is not to limit our praying in any way, but to enhance moments available to us. Even as Jesus prayed in a moment of time for those who crucified Him, *"Father, forgive them, for they do not know what they do"* (Luke 23:34), we can call out to God in behalf of others. Waiting for the Lord to give us big chunks of time to devote to extended intercessory prayer sessions might delay God's answer for the people involved.

The framework supporting the tapestry of this book comes from a poem I wrote during my early twenties which I titled, "Traveling on My Knees." At the time, I was a student at a

Bible training facility in Waxahachie, Texas. I felt it was God's calling for me to become an intercessor for Him. "Traveling on my knees" refers to the attitude of prayer we are called upon to maintain. At times we do kneel and pray fervently. At many other times, however, our hearts assume a kneeling position whenever and wherever prompted by the Holy Spirit. Although I wrote the poem during the 1950s, it continues to express to me the prayer opportunities we all have. I refer to it as God's constant reminder of what I, and every other ordinary person, can do for Him.

It was while Jesus went about all the cities and villages teaching, preaching, and healing that He saw the needs of the multitudes and was moved with compassion. Matthew 9:38 relates that out of this setting He commanded us, His Church, to pray for laborers to enter His harvest. He desires that all learn the joy of prayerful traveling.

Laborers for Christ are not limited to missionaries in foreign lands, preachers in pulpits, and teachers in Christian schools. Every child of God who knows and loves Him can enter His harvest field through prayer, traveling in the heart as well as on the knees.

Although I have not written from an in-depth theology of prayer, I believe that what I have written from a practical standpoint is theologically correct. I do not write as someone who knows absolutely everything about prayer, nor do I speak as an authority of the church. Like you, I continue to learn daily at our Father's feet. But during these past sixty-plus years of relationship with the Lord Jesus Christ, I have walked through varied life experiences, interruptions if you will, that have served to tutor me.

My desire is to share with you some lessons I have learned in my own personal school of prayer. How I thank God for those times of instruction and worship. I continue to treasure meaningful moments in prayer, developing my personal intimacy with Christ. It is out of that intimate relationship that I have learned the value of ongoing, prayerful intercession, praying for others as I move about my daily responsibilities, praying in a moment of time for people in need.

May you glean from these chapters and from your study of God's Word those strengths and strategies you seek for the journey of a lifetime. May God lead you in applying them to your special times with the Lord, those times which I have chosen to call *moments of intercession* in the midst of managing life's interruptions.

—Sandra G. C. Drake

CHAPTER ONE

Embarking

"The world is a book,
And those who do not travel
Read only a page."

—Saint Augustine

> *"Last night I took a journey*
> *To a land far 'cross the seas;*
> *I didn't go by boat or plane;*
> *I traveled on my knees."*

Traveling on my knees might seem like an impossible way to see the world. However, there is much more to the story. So, let me explain what I mean.

Embarking on the journey of a lifetime can be a giant task. I remember such a journey back in 1962. It was my first trip to Africa as a new missionary. When my husband, my daughter, and I boarded the freighter in New York Harbor, I recall how huge that ship looked. I watched the giant cranes load our packing crates, appliances, and even our Chevrolet truck into the hold of that great ship. I thought about the voyage ahead all the way from New York City to Ghana, West Africa. We felt like we had already had quite a trip driving from Texas to New York. Calculating what the rest of the trip would be like was beyond my comprehension.

Good instruction comes from an African proverb: *"The day on which one starts out is not the time to start one's preparation."* Embarking comes only after much planning and preparation. We had packed crates. We filled 55-gallon drums with personal goods and

> *As you begin to intercede, start with the basics, where you are at this moment in time.*

provisions. We had prayed. We had raised funds to provide for our ministries on the field. So a good part of embarking on the journey was eased by the fact that we had done everything we could to prepare ourselves for that moment. But how can we prepare ourselves for life's journey?

Although starting on the journey may look like a formidable task, God helps us prepare for it. The key is that we not try to take on the whole journey at once. It's like the question, "How do you eat an elephant?" The answer is, "One bite at a time."

Embarking might be compared to baking a cake from scratch. You start with flour, eggs, sugar, salt, and baking powder. In other words, you start with the basics, adding one ingredient after another until the cake is ready for the oven.

So it is with a prayer journey. As you begin to intercede, you start with the basics, where you are at this moment in time. You pray from your own frame of reference. God understands your age, your talents and abilities, your physical and mental capabilities, and where you are in your relationship to Him. Start with the basics, and build your life in intercessory prayer. Let me give you a personal example.

As a young person, I loved basketball. I had grown up in Fort Wayne, Indiana, a city which once was spotlighted in a national magazine as "Hoop Happy Town." Girls did not play on organized basketball teams in those days. However, I loved shooting baskets with my only sibling, my brother Gene. During seventh grade in my rural school, there was a sharpshooting contest for girls and boys. This involved shooting the basketball from various locations on the court. The one with the most points won. How thrilled I was one year to win a trophy naming me County Sharpshooter.

In the seventh grade, I hadn't yet found the Lord as my Savior. I did not know that He could use my love for basketball to propel me into prayer opportunities. Yet that's exactly what the Lord did.

More than forty years later while serving in ministry at our national headquarters in Springfield, Missouri, I attended a basketball tournament involving local college teams. Several days later I discovered the team rosters in my purse. I felt impressed of the Holy Spirit to keep them. Those rosters contained names of students who played on three college teams. I knew that college students often struggle with their schedules, class work, and finances. I put the lists in my Bible as well as in my personal organizer. Glancing at them from time to time, calling their names in prayer during moments of intercession, those lists became part of my weekly prayer schedule.

When you intercede in prayer, you pray on behalf of others. You are trying to step into their shoes and feel what they are feeling. You seek God for answers as though the burdens were your own.

God knew my heart and my interest in basketball. He knew each of those players and what they were facing. He knew how to touch my heart with their needs. What a joy to pray for them at various moments throughout the week! While praying one particular morning, my heart was burdened for a certain player. Later that morning I learned that his father had died suddenly, and that student was traveling home in great sorrow. I was glad I had been obedient to the Lord's prompting to pray over those rosters. I felt He was hearing my prayers for that young man.

When you intercede in prayer, you pray on behalf of others. You are trying to step into their shoes and feel what they are feeling. You seek God for answers as though the burdens were your own. In other prayers you might petition God for specific needs you have, but in intercessory prayer you lift to Him the needs of someone else.

Multitudes of people in your world, with a magnitude of needs in their lives, give ample reason to spend time in prayer. Our Creator God is so infinite that He can see the whole world at once and can hear the cries of our hearts. There will be times that a burden you feel for a friend, family member, or total stranger will fill your heart. While you work at your desk, run the cash register, or feed the baby, you silently cry out to God for His intervention. Those momentary, fervent prayers matter much to those you are praying for and to God who prompts you to be obedient.

Pondering the difference between a mountain of time and a moment of time, may bring questions your mind. *How can I possibly pray enough to be effective? How can an intercessory prayer moment make a difference?* A moment is a comparatively brief period of time. One dictionary defines it as a time of excellence; a time of importance in influence or effect. Some synonyms are "importance," "consequence," "significance." Certainly praying for those in need is a matter of excellence and one of importance in God's eyes. It can also be a time of consequence and significance. You might still question how you can be effective in praying in brief moments. Doesn't it take more intensity than that? Shouldn't such praying be laced with high emotion that carries it to great lengths?

I would say yes to these questions. The more you pray, the more you want to pray, and the more intense your prayer becomes. Remember, however, that we are talking about embarking. We are talking about starting our journey in prayer. We start from scratch with this moment in time.

The first line of the poem at the beginning of the chapter says, *"Last night I took a journey to a land far 'cross the seas. I didn't go by boat or plane; I traveled on my knees."* That could have been the picture of someone laboring all night in prayer. Or possibly someone who experiences a dramatic moment of intercession before God. Maybe there was a dream followed by an awakening from sleep. During those moments prayer was made. A person who has never ventured more than 100 miles from home can experience travel in prayer to a distant land, even in the middle of the night. With God such things are possible.

Have you ever been startled by someone's name suddenly coming to your mind? Why do you think that happened? Maybe you were cooking dinner, changing a tire, or driving down the street. What did you do with that moment? Did you pass it off as a strange occurrence?

It could be that God was giving you that name at that moment for you to take to Him in prayer. Richard Foster says, *"We are responsible before God to pray for those God brings into our circle of nearness"[1].* You never know what circumstances people might be in at the time you are thinking of them. Even though you might not be able to stop what you are doing, you can certainly pray for them with

> *You never know what circumstances people might be in at the time you are thinking of them.*

focus, compassion, and concern. You have just experienced a moment of intercession.

To be an intercessor, you must be available to God. You must learn to think on Him and His Word. Keep your heart tuned to His prompting as well as to people and events around you. Perhaps that is what Paul meant when he said we should pray without ceasing. That could involve any amount of time.

If you desire to pray, but haven't been praying for an hour a day, don't start by trying to fill up an hour with prayer. Spend moments developing your relationship with the Lord. As you go about your day, thank Him for who He is as well as what He has done. Become intimately related to Him with a ready

---

[1] *The Prayer-Centered Life* by Dudley J. Delffs, p. 92.

response of worship and prayer in your heart. Let Him fill your thoughts, desires and your concerns with Himself. Then you can experience the true meaning of prayer, feeling His heartbeat and mind-set for the needs at hand. As the Apostle Paul expressed in Philippians 2:5, *"Let this mind be in you which was also in Christ Jesus."*

Prayer involves reading God's Word. In fact, many prayers in the Bible can be read as prayers from the heart. Read a Psalm and a Proverb daily. Meditate for a few moments on what those verses mean in your life and in the lives of those around you. Ask the Lord to help you internalize the concepts set forth, and to ponder His holiness. By so doing, your heart will be available for the Holy Spirit's prompting at any moment of the day. Remember that prayer is not something to do only when you or someone else is in need. Prayer is more than a wish list. It is more than praying for those closest to you, *"our four and no more."* Prayer is something you do daily to know Him better. Prayer moves you close to God for you to see things from His perspective. He draws you to Himself to submit your finite will to His infinite plan.

A great part of prayer is worship, or "worthship." Joseph L. Garlington expresses this beautifully in his book, *The Pattern of Things in Heaven.* He speaks of prayer as an action of entering the awesome presence of God and yielding ourselves to Him with the admission that He

> *The more you pray, the more you want to pray, and the more intense your prayer becomes.*

is the greater One. Garlington says that praise is extending our hands to God, and worship is bowing our faces to the ground. These are attitudes of the heart we must strive to maintain throughout our daily activities.

7

As you draw close to God, you ascribe worth to Him. As you seek His face, you let Him know you are dependent on Him. Let your intercession grow out of your delight in worshipping Him. Before you know it, you may spend five, ten, fifteen minutes or more. However, don't make the amount of time your focus. Focus on Christ, His Word, and the joy you find in Him.

A schoolteacher once told me that if I would take care of the minutes, the hours would take care of themselves. She was talking about activities at school and relationships I had. I believe this is true in prayer as it is in all areas of life.

Martin Luther wrote, *"Prayer is the most important thing in my life. If I should neglect prayer for a single day, I should lose a great deal of faith."*[2]

I came into a personal relationship with the Lord at the age of sixteen. With no background in prayer, I had to embark upon the journey, starting from scratch. One of the first things I did after salvation was to attend the weekly prayer meetings at our church where people gathered specifically to pray for others. I watched Paul and Evelyn Ayers, along with Johnny and Ruby Southworth, and Mrs. Habig. As they felt burdened for someone, I saw their tears flow and heard their groans and intercessions. Their songs of victory gladdened my heart as they praised God for lifting the burdens under which they had labored in prayer. This was a genuine school of prayer at a time when I desperately needed to learn.

I will always be grateful for those seasoned saints who served as my instructors in intercession. They took me from where I was as a sixteen-year-old new Christian, and helped me develop my own personal intimacy with Christ. From there I learned to launch out in sustained prayer for others.

---

[2] *The Speaker's Sourcebook,* compiled by Eleanor L. Dean, p. 192.

Two years after being saved, I journeyed to Waxahachie, Texas to attend Southwestern Bible Institute. There I was exposed to a whole new set of circumstances, especially to the thrill of missions. My world began to expand as I studied and heard speakers tell about the regions beyond. On Missions Day each Wednesday, I attended the morning and noon prayer meetings. I went to the chapel early in the morning to pray for those who were on my missions prayer list. Those were not long, extended prayer sessions, but moments of intense focus as we called out names of missionaries and the countries where they worked. From those prayer experiences I wrote the poem, "Traveling on My Knees."

As I struggled to rise early week after week to be in the prayer meetings, I felt keenly that one day I might be on the mission field somewhere and need urgent prayer. Much to my surprise and somewhat dismay, that's exactly what happened. Eventually I took a journey to Africa, a land far across the seas.

During my Bible training, I became engaged to a fine young man. Sid Goodwin had grown up in West Africa and felt a call to minister in that area. We married, graduated from Bible College and went to Ghana, West Africa, as missionaries. At the time we arrived in Africa, we had a darling blond-headed three-year-old daughter named Gwenda.

Little did we know what a short span Sid's missionary career would cover. Just six weeks after arriving for our first term, we confronted the task of burying Sid on African soil.

A tragic accident occurred at our Christmas Eve service. We had traveled to the village of Tili in far Northern Ghana where Africans had gathered by the hundreds to welcome the missionary kid who had grown up there and was now returning with his wife and child. Sid was severely burned when a portable generator which had been placed on our pickup tailgate suddenly exploded. He and a Ghanaian were trying to adjust the lighting for the event. Sid was the only one trapped in the camper which covered the pickup bed.

Extensive burns held him at death's door for one week while national Christians and missionaries cried out to God for His healing. Sid's passing on January 1, 1963 truly overwhelmed everyone, and confronted us with serious questions about the sovereignty of God. Our lives were traumatically interrupted, but we knew beyond a shadow of a doubt that God was in charge of it all. We determined to abide in the peace of God which Sid had exemplified throughout that whole ordeal.

During those difficult days I learned firsthand how powerful and far-reaching intercessory prayer can be. I felt the confirmation of what I had written earlier about traveling on my knees; that prayer knows neither geographical boundaries nor chronological restrictions. I felt strongly the reciprocal prayers of Southwestern students and others who took time to pray for a missionary in need. How long each one prayed for me was not a consideration at that time. What I did consider, however, was that someone took powerful moments and directed prayer to God for me and my family.

> *Sid's passing on January 1, 1963, truly overwhelmed everyone, and we were confronted with serious questions about the sovereignty of God.*

Twenty years as a widow and single parent presented many opportunities for me to continue the development of my personal devotion in prayer and moments of intercession for others. My growing daughter kept me close to my Lord as I grappled daily with parental decisions and desires for the best life I could provide for her. God took me where I was as a teenager, prepared me for embarking on my journey, and walked with me through the basics. I learned that even in tragedy God would meet me at my point of need and that of my daughter as well.

Sometimes you may feel confused at what God is trying to do with your life. In the natural your circumstances don't make sense. Be assured, though, that through every valley experience, you face the powerful truth that He never leaves you nor forsakes you. And when you feel like you are at the end of your rope, He touches someone else in the Body of Christ whose prayer helps you tie a knot and hang on. Every day is a new opportunity for you to embark on your journey and to start from scratch. Hear the words of Lamentations 3:22-23: *"Through the Lord's mercies we are not consumed. Because His compassions fail not. They are new every morning. Great is Your faithfulness."*

God rewarded the faith of the Children of Israel as the Jews were returning from Babylonian exile. The book of Ezra tells of the dangerous 900-mile journey they had to make through an area infested with bandits and warring factions. Although God's people had no military protection, He rewarded their faith with an uneventful journey as told in Ezra 8:31. The trip took about four months to complete, and the people averaged seven to eight miles per day. They did not abandon the journey just because things were suddenly tough. They plodded on.

We too must act in a way which is consistent with the faith we proclaim. We know that life's journey will be fraught with unavoidable struggles and interruptions. Yet, we cling to the One who will always be faithful!

Maybe you feel inadequate in your present practice of prayer. You doubt that anything will change in this regard. Cheer up! I have good news for you. Right now is a new opportunity to make a fresh start. God wants your fellowship and calls to you right where you are, even in the midst of monumental interruptions.

Take time with God today. Expect an overwhelming sense of His presence as you yield your life to Him. God has some amazing adventures for you in the arena of prayer; adventures you can experience throughout the moments of your day/

Someone has said, *"A short prayer will reach the throne - - if you don't live too far away."* We must stay close to God.

Only eternity will reveal what you might accomplish for His glory as you meet Him and He meets you during those moments of intercession. He simply asks that you start where you are and prepare to embark on the journey ahead, the journey of a lifetime, as you travel on your knees.

GOD'S CALL

In the stillness of the midnight;
In the quiet early morn;
In the sunset hours at even;
After daily cares have worn;

In those times of sweet surrender
When my soul draws near to God,
I perceive His gentle leading
O'er the pathway I have trod.

Then it is His call comes clearer,
Ever ringing in my heart;
Striking chords of deep submission;
Chords which peace and joy impart.

In those times of calm assurance
When all other voices fade,
I renew the consecration
Which on bended knee I made.

Although other plans may falter;
Many dreams may come and go;
Though the world may think me foolish
As the Word of God I sow;

To the task of teaching others
Of God's Love and Grace so free;
I will serve Him where He beckons;
Here at home or 'cross the sea.

—Sandra G. C. Drake

CHAPTER TWO

Sightseeing

"One doesn't discover new lands
without consenting to lose sight of the shore
for a very long time."

—André Gide

> *"I saw so many people there*
> *In deepest depths of sin,*
> *And Jesus told me I should go,*
> *That there were souls to win."*

After the tragedy in northern Ghana, Gwenda and I moved to the central Ashanti area where my in-laws, Homer and Thelma Goodwin and their two younger children, John and Nova, were serving. We looked around us and realized that we could involve ourselves with ministry in this large area.

I met weekly with the women of the Kumasi church in their prayer and Bible Study meetings. Soon I also saw the need to assist the young people in their Christ's Ambassador meetings. Before long, Gwenda and I were ministering throughout the Ashanti villages where she stood on a chair by my side, leading the villagers in singing and worship. We were greatly encouraged and fulfilled to see many responding to the message of salvation as the Word of God impacted people's lives.

To see ourselves as prayer partners with Jesus is a snapshot we want to keep before us.

However, after almost two years in Ghana, our family felt it best that we all return to the States for a season of furlough and opportunity to seek God further concerning what the future might hold. It was difficult to leave the wonderful Ghanaian people, but our sights were set on following the next steps the Lord might have for us. What a faithful God we serve!

After six years of traveling in ministry, getting further education, being ordained as a minister of the Gospel, and my re-commissioning as a single missionary with a child, Gwenda and I journeyed to the country of Tanzania, East Africa. There

I enjoyed teaching in the Bible training school in Arusha with wonderful missionary colleagues, and Gwenda eventually attended a nearby boarding school. We loved being back in Africa.

Traveling enlarges our horizons. It helps us see the big picture of what life is all about. Many new sights await us on our journey. Mixing with people of other cultural backgrounds and geographical settings provides an education we cannot get from a classroom lecture or book. Tourists seem to take on a culture all their own. Loaded with cameras, tripods, recorders, they determine not to miss a thing. In so doing, they put an interesting touch on the landscape.

While we served as missionaries in Tanzania, my daughter became a teenager. She and her friends had a favorite pastime. They thought it great sport to go down to the hotel in our small town to watch tourists arriving and departing at the hotel. Many dressed in expensive safari outfits, including hats, to go out and sit all day in a tour van. Of course, cameras were visible everywhere so they could capture the most exciting shots of wildlife in the African bush. They were ready to see the sights.

The missionary kids were at an advantage. Because they were familiar with the locale, they could see the big picture of what the tourists would be doing and where they would be going. The tourists, however, could see only one snapshot at a time because with every move they made they were charting new waters. As travelers on the journey of life, I wonder how big our picture is. How much do we see of the world around us? How far-reaching are our prayers? If we are not careful, we can allow our world to become quite small.

We confine our areas of concern to family and home, close friends, our workplace and colleagues, and our church family. Because these are familiar to us, it is easy to feel drawn to them in prayer. It is easy to pray for their protection, provision, and profit. We must pray for all of these, but it is possible to limit our praying in ways that God never intended. Maybe we need to see a bigger picture of what prayer is all about.

Jesus told us to go into all the world and preach the gospel to every creature. He also told us to pray without ceasing. Something big must be going on to include the whole world, all people, at all times. That something big is God's love for the world. He loved mankind so much that He gave His only son, Jesus, to redeem all from sin. When we pray, we touch the world for God. God calls us to see the big picture and develop our part in it.

Richard Halverson once said, *"Intercession is truly universal work for the Christian. No place is closed to intercessory prayer; no continent-no nation-no organization-no city-no office. There is no power on earth that can keep intercession out."*

John 17 gives us a view of the Son praying to the Father. Verse 8 reveals Jesus' prayer for all who received Him: *"I have given to them the words which You have given Me and they have received them, and have known surely that I came forth from You; and they have believed that You sent Me."*

Verses 20-21 let us know that the picture includes everybody who will receive Him: *"I do not pray for these alone, but also for those who will believe in Me through their word; that they all may be one, as You, Father, are in Me, and I in You; that they also may be one in Us, that the world may know that You sent Me."*

Do you get the picture? According to these verses, the most important thing we can do in life is to find Jesus Christ as Lord and Savior. How different this is from the world's perspective. We constantly face the bombardment of infomercials that tell us fame, fortune, and a fabulous body are the only avenues to real success and fulfillment. Even in the church we sometimes get the message that real life is found only in good health and great wealth.

Look at Jesus' prayer again: *"That they also may be one in Us, that the world may believe that You sent Me."* God's goal for mankind expands the definition of fulfillment. He is not willing that any should perish, but that all would come to oneness or completeness in Christ. Total fulfillment is realized when God's people are united in Him, and the illustration of that unity draws the world to Him.

The big picture is that Christ died for the whole world. He prays for us and for all who come after us. The Word says that He always lives to make intercession for those who come to God through Him (Hebrews 7:25). Because He always intercedes, we are His prayer partners whenever we pray. To see ourselves as prayer partners with Jesus is a snapshot we want to keep before us. We should keep it at the very front of our spiritual album.

As Jesus' prayer partners, we must keep in mind how much God loves the lost. Without a fervor for the lost, our prayers will not carry much weight. *"As by one man's disobedience many were made sinners, so also by one Man's obedience many will be made righteous"* (Romans 5:19).

Think of the price Jesus paid to carry out the kind of obedience required of God the Father. I wonder what kind of insightful obedience God expects of us. How many might be made righteous if we would seize opportunities to pray in a moment of time that the lost all around us might be saved!

You may never preach an evangelistic message from the pulpit. You may not be bold in giving public testimony of your faith. You can, however get close enough to Jesus to feel His compassion for the lost. In so doing, your prayers will take on new vision. Your spiritual eyes will be opened. You'll have a new passion and anticipation for people to be drawn to Him. Listen to Paul's compassionate declaration in Romans 9:1-3: *"I tell the truth in Christ. I am not lying; my conscience also bearing me witness in the Holy Spirit, that I have great sorrow and continual grief in my heart. For I could wish that I myself were accursed from Christ for my brethren, my countrymen according to the flesh."*

It would be to our advantage to pray for the kind of heart we read about in the Bible. John's gospel tells us about desire for winning the lost. *"You did not choose Me, but I chose you and appointed you that you should go and bear fruit, and that your fruit should remain, that whatever you ask the Father in My name He may give you"* (John 15:16)

Across denominational lines, God's people are finding creative ways to partner together in prayer evangelism. A Baptist church in Oregon became so caught up in the prayer movement that God burdened their hearts for their entire rural community. The pastor encouraged them in that they observe their community and its inhabitants.

Not only did they have many prayer meetings at the church each week, but also groups of people walked the school playgrounds and athletic fields while praying. They worked out a plan of providing lists of teachers, administrators, and students so names could be called in prayer. Those were moments of intercession in action. They prayed for wisdom, protection, adherence to God's laws of righteousness and for those in the schools to experience salvation through Christ.

This same church sent groups of people to pray at government office buildings to seek God for His guidance in their community. Because they sought God for a plan of action, He showed them a plan that would work for them. That small church, in a town with a population of 1,700 grew to have a weekly attendance of over 1,300. It is no wonder the church became known as "the praying church."

How many stories have we heard of praying mothers who refused to give up on their children? Praying daily for thirty or forty years takes persistence and lion-like faith. These mothers felt the agony of what would be missing in heaven if family ties were broken. A vision of eternity motivated them to keep praying for their lost children. May God give us all such a vision.

Houses of Prayer, developed by Al Vander Griend of Grand Rapids, Michigan, have become a worldwide prayer movement. Many have walked their neighborhood praying for each home as they walk. Christians have reached out to their neighbors to let their neighbors know they are praying for them and inviting prayer requests. Every home in the neighborhood has encountered God's love and presence, and many neighbors have responded by expressing their desire to know Christ.

One of the door hangers left on a neighbor's house reads, *"Your house has been totally surrounded and covered with prayer. You may notice an increase in peacefulness and encouragement in the next several weeks. We've been gathering on a regular basis to pray for you and your household. Please let us know if there is something we can pray specifically about for you, or for someone you care about. There is power in prayer."*

> I really believe we must go as far as we can see, and when we get there, undoubtedly we will see farther.

According to the National Day of Prayer Task Force, there was a measurable drop in crime in the city of Philadelphia during May 1997. It wasn't due to increased police protection or any new emphasis on law and order. It wasn't that the lawbreakers had been rounded up and put in jail. Nor had the local delinquents and troublemakers gone on vacation. The cause of this decrease in the crime rate was a direct result of the earnest and focused prayers of concerned community residents.

The 1998 Pray USA emphasis marshaled the forces of millions of Americans for forty days of synchronized fervent prayer and fasting to *"Pray America Back to God."* In the planning materials there were suggestions for praying through the phone book. Different groups in a town or community took different sections of the phone book, assigning individuals to pray momentarily over each name listed. What a task! It seemed almost impossible. Can you imagine, however, what could happen if every person listed in every phone book received individual specific prayer?

Thank God that creative prayer initiatives are being launched on an ongoing basis for our United States of America and the world at large! Oh, how we need a new touch of God's righteousness throughout the land!

We must realize that prayer cannot and must not be done in a frivolous, haphazard way. We must plan and strategize our efforts to intercede for others. This is the only way we can make moments of intercession count for eternity.

Jesus Himself made careful plans. He spoke of ninety-nine sheep and His diligent search for one that was lost. He planned the approach of his visit with Zacchaeus. He prepared Himself to deal with fishermen, farmers, and folks of all occupations. Employing various tactics, He impacted lives one by one as well as in great gatherings of people.

A former pastor asked our congregation to write down the names of "Seven for Heaven." He challenged us to list seven people that we would like to see won to the Lord by the end of the year. At first, I deliberated much over whose names to write down. Then, as I took pen and paper and knelt before the Lord, faces began to appear in my mind's eye. Some of them I didn't know by name. I had to write simply, "The young man who works at the gas station," or, "The lady at the grocery store checkout lane."

What amazed me about this process was that the more I prayed for those named, the more desirous I was of seeing them in eternity. I began to think of them as living souls rather than people I barely knew. They came to mind at various times, and I directed a prayer to God. Included in that prayer was a cry for direction that I might show them God's love more openly.

The Lord has many people He would like us to touch for Him. Our pictures get bigger and bigger as we reach out in prayer. We need to take an awareness posture and observe the signposts all around us. See the man walking dejectedly down

> *Ask God to invade the life of someone you encounter today.*

the street with shoulders slumped. Look intently at the young woman heavy with child whose car just broke down while storm clouds are threatening. While praying for those we meet day-by-day and moment-by-moment, we invite God to do something very significant in other lives as well as ours.

Ask God to invade the life of someone you encounter today. You may pray something like, *"Whatever it takes, Lord, touch them with Your presence. Help them to consider the real meaning of life. Give them a tender heart to respond to your Holy Spirit. And help me to understand what you might be telling me to do as a part of that process. In Jesus' name. Amen."*

Don't let your world degenerate into a tiny one consisting only of self. Lift up your eyes and see the sights around you.

Internalize Christ's command to go into all the world and preach the gospel to every creature. It isn't enough to satisfy only your own personal prayer requests. If you are a genuine disciple of the Lord Jesus, your horizons in prayer will surely become the journey of a lifetime.

Frank Herbert once said, *"Without new experiences, something inside us sleeps. The sleeper must awaken."* I really believe we should go as far as we can see, and when we get there, undoubtedly, we will see farther.

All the world is a mighty big picture, but individuals in that world may live just around the corner. Each one is a candidate for your moments of intercession. Who knows? God may use you to make it count for eternity!

I AM A MISSIONARY

Called of God,
Committed to the Task,
Commissioned by the Church.

My calling is lofty and sacred;
My commitment has worldwide thrust;
My commission comes through people and places.

I travel far and wide.
I stand before large crowds.
I report uplifting victories.

Often laughing;
Other times singing,
Or sometimes weeping.

I am a missionary.

I AM A PERSON —

Having needs,
Harboring fears,
Hurting with loneliness.

Reaching out, I want to bless.
Reflecting faith, to intercede.
Reciting truth, to edify.

When I miss the goal,
When my vision dims,
When my body tires, I

Call on God,
Commune with friends,
Claim the Word.

I am a Person.

Please be sensitive to my calling,
Sustaining in my commitment,
Supportive of my commission.

I Am A Missionary.

I Am A Person.

I Am Depending on You!

—Sandra G. C. Drake

CHAPTER THREE

Enabling

**"If I cannot do great things,
I will do small things
In a great way."**

—J. F. Clarke

> *"But I said, 'Jesus, I can't go*
> *And work with such as these.'*
> *He answered quickly, 'Yes, you can*
> *By traveling on your knees.'"*

When I served as a volunteer chaplain for the Evangel University Lady Crusaders, I remember vividly how often I reminded the team of the "Ten Finger Sermon" found in Philippians 4:13: *"I can do all things through Christ who strengthens me."* Whether they were facing something in their personal lives or a play that looked impossible on the basketball court, this scripture seemed to let them know that God would enable them to succeed. This was one of those life lessons which came through to me whenever I was tempted to say, "I can't do that!"

Is this sometimes your first response when you feel God calling on you for a certain task? Maybe the call comes through a Sunday- School teacher or church -education director. Maybe it comes through your pastor. Perhaps it is the choir director or a member of the youth group who reaches for your help.

Moses could identify with your feelings for when God called him to lead His people out of Egyptian bondage, he answered, *"Who am I that I should go to Pharaoh and that I should bring the children of Israel out of Egypt?"* (Exodus 3:11). Later he simply said, *"Lord, please send somebody else,"* (Exodus 4:13). We would interpret this as saying, *"Lord, I'm not good enough. Someone else can do it better. Call them."*

None of us is adequate for God's task. No one works hard enough or prays long enough to do a thorough job. Your thought that someone else can do it better is valid. But that's beside the point. Another person might see the task as too difficult also or might not agree to be involved. God has a plan for you and me at this moment in time. He doesn't ask how capable we are.

Rather, how available are we? How willing are we to let Him work through us?

William Booth said, *"The greatness of a man's power is the measure of his surrender. How much of ourselves will we give to God?"*

When we ponder the vast expanse of our world and the needs represented in it, we can become so overwhelmed that we feel prayer is useless. Actually, we develop guilt feelings because of our being inadequate, and the inadequacy consumes us. We feel like the proverbial kitten that fell into a barrel of milk and cried, *"Oh, that I had a capacity equal to my opportunity."*

Each of us can appropriate God's message to Moses, *"I am who I AM! Thus you shall say to the children of Israel, 'I AM has sent me to you'*

. . .The Lord God of your fathers, the God of Abraham, the God of Isaac, and the God of Jacob has sent me to you" (Exodus 3:14, 15). Moses learned that the God who calls is the God who enables and provides a way through which he could do all things.

Do you sometimes ask yourself, "What's wrong with me? Why do I seem to run out of words when I talk to God? Why can't I pray for

> *Moses learned that the God who calls is the God who enables.*

long stretches of time like other Christians I know? Does God love them more than He loves me?"

Such questions can be born of guilt and inadequacy you bring upon yourself. Knowing it is the Christian's duty and God's command to pray, you may feel guilty about not praying. When you do pray, you feel it's never enough. Maybe you compare yourself with those who speak of prayer as a peaceful, uplifting experience. Again guilt sets in because you find it complex and difficult. What is the answer to this enigma?

Perhaps we try too hard to make it happen. Why do we insist on playing God? Sometimes when we pray we have a solution worked out in our mind and we feel we must assist God in bringing it about. We might feel we know the person or the hazard and difficulty of a situation even better than He does.

Relax. It is not your responsibility to make anything happen. God is eternal, without beginning and without ending. He knows all. He sees all. He needs you only as a yielded vessel through whom He can work as your enabler.

In Romans 8:26-27, Paul speaks to this issue, *"The Spirit also helps in our weaknesses. For we do not know what we should pray for as we ought, but the Spirit Himself makes intercession for us with groaning which cannot be uttered. Now He who searches the hearts knows what the mind of the Spirit is because He makes intercession for the saints according to the will of God."* The Holy Spirit knows exactly what God's will is, and you can leave the matter with Him.

God gave His Son on the cross that you might approach Him, not in your merit, but in His. This is where faith kicks in. You not only give Him your requests and leave the matter in His hands, but you trust Him while soaking in the pure joy of His presence.

Working with volunteers who answered phones in a national prayer center, I have seen over and over the tendency to fix someone else's problem. This is an automatic response from those who want to help others. As Christians, we feel obligated to do so and feel so inadequate when we fail in our attempts. To fail is to admit weakness and lack of God's anointing (so we think). Maybe this is why it is hard for us to understand the merit of interceding for only a minute. We feel we must pray long and hard in every situation, for surely God will not answer unless we demonstrate power and persistence.

As you study God's Word, though, you will see that He simply asks you to come. *"Come unto Me, all you who labor and are heavy laden, and I will give you rest"* (Matthew 11:28).

No matter how pure your intentions may be, only Christ Himself can minister rest and wholeness to those who come. It is He who is able to "fix" all problems. Your part is to bring Him those needs in prayer moment by moment.

Hebrews 4:16 says we are to come to God neither hesitantly nor timidly. Rather, *"Come boldly to the throne of grace, that we may obtain mercy and find grace to help in time of need."* Coming boldly does not mean bursting into God's presence with great demands. It does not mean coming brashly. We must never come with the idea of manipulating Him and trying to change His mind about what He has said.

Leonard Ravenhill wrote, *"Prayer is not an argument with God to persuade Him to move things our way, but an exercise by which we are enabled by His Spirit to move ourselves His way."* He is God, the Sovereign of the Universe, and He knows what is best for us. We must trust His justice as well as His abundant provisions.

I am reminded of what I heard Henry Blackaby say at a meeting of the Denominational Prayer Leaders Network: *"So often when we hear God, we assume He is wanting us to do something for Him. But that's not the case. He is announcing to us what He is going to do. We are to manage our lives to join with God in what He is preparing to do."*

Don't we usually respond to God's promptings by making great plans for what we want to accomplish? Why can't we agree with what God wants to do and spend our energies aligning our purposes with His? How can we expect God to bless what doesn't please Him? As Oswald Chambers once stated, *"We do the things that can be tabulated, but we will not intercede."*

Prayer is the opportunity to experience the fullness of God. He fortifies us with His spiritual strength and helps us to feel what He feels. Prayer is a relationship with God which affects our relationships with other people. It is a response of obedience in patience as we wait before Him. Prayer is a redefinition of our priorities in the light of God's perspective. He asks us to come for spiritual nourishment, equipping and enabling that we might be able to face the task ahead.

Dr. Terry Tekyl of Renewal Ministries has said, *"So often we wind Christianity too tight. We have a knack for making our relationship with God through prayer a burden. If it makes us feel guilty, we avoid it. But of all things in the Christian life, prayer is the one thing we should enjoy the most. It is a delight to communicate with the Father. It is our point of contact with the Omnipotent One."*

One reason we find it hard to come to God is that we feel uncomfortable expressing our need to anyone. Surely, as grown-ups we can take care of ourselves. We like to think of ourselves as professionals, not beggars or little children. We prop up tough images of ourselves which we try to project to others. We fear what people might say if they know we have a need or a weakness of some kind. After all, as Christians we are supposed to experience victory in every aspect of our lives, aren't we?

On the other hand, we might be too hasty to talk with family and acquaintances before we talk with God. Since they are human too, they can understand feelings of reluctance and shortcomings. People who know us might help us justify feelings of inadequacy rather than confess we have need of God's help.

Yet, confessing our need is exactly what God wants us to do. A French proverb declares, *"Prayer is a cry of hope."*

G. Campbell Morgan admitted, *"That I know my own weakness is a sign of my own strength."*

Only when I come to Him in weakness can He provide strength from His vast resource.

Read the account of Solomon in 1 Kings, chapter 3.

After Solomon was made king, the Lord appeared to him in a dream to ask him what he needed. Solomon felt in his heart that he was a little child and did not know how to go out or come in. His prayer was for God to give him an understanding heart to discern between good and evil in leading his people. The Bible tells us that this request pleased the Lord, and Solomon's desire was granted. When he awakened from his dream, all Israel saw that he had the wisdom of God and administered justice.

God exhorts us to come humbly and hopefully to our loving Heavenly Father. *"Let the little children come to Me, and do not forbid them; for of such is the kingdom of God. Assuredly, I say to you, whoever does not receive the kingdom of God as a little child will by no means enter it"* (Mark 10:14-15). *"As a little child"* speaks of a childlike trust, not immaturity. Nowhere does the Bible exhort us to be childish or to take on a little child's mind-set. But there are qualities in children that we could emulate when coming to the Lord.

Little children abound with trust. They like to be with friends. They thrive on relationships that encourage and comfort them. They love the feeling of intimacy with those stronger than they. This is the kind of relationship God wants us to have with Him. His Word tells us that He is a *"friend who sticks closer than a brother"* (Proverbs 18:24). Prayer is God's way for us to communicate with this Friend. No one can equal His love, strength, and understanding of our needs.

Not only do children trust, but they anticipate the joy of a special moment before it arrives. Witness a child going to a circus. See the jumping, clapping, giggling, and general excitement in anticipation of what is ahead. Fear and hesitancy have no part in the scenario. The child's attitude exudes triumph!

Try anticipating your prayer time with childlike enthusiasm. Don't try to keep score on the length of your prayers. Don't fret over not praying enough. Instead of playing God and trying to figure out how and what He might do, try coming to Him with an expectation of simply delighting in His presence. Believe that He is able and through Him you will be enabled to touch others as He directs.

Recognize that prayer is a cry of dependency, a relationship of intimacy, and an attitude of expectancy. Hear your Heavenly Father calling you to come. Trust Him that He knows best. Free yourself from an outsized ego that refuses to admit the need for God's help. Let your acknowledgment of weakness serve you with His inner strength. As W. S. Bowden once said, *"Prayer is weakness leaning on Omnipotence.*

I remember the weakness I felt as a child when a neighbor's Shetland pony threw me through a barbed wire fence. The neighbor insisted that I get right back on that pony. He said if I did not, I would never feel enabled to ride again. Well, I guess he was right because I did get back on and continued riding throughout my teens and twenties; even helping that same neighbor break other horses.

This was a good lesson in "never quitting:" one which I remembered later as I contemplated a quotation from S. D. Gordon. *"Prayer strikes the winning blow; service is simply picking up the pieces."*

More than once did I experience God's enabling at a time when I felt I just could not do what was expected of me. During the time we were home from Ghana, I studied at West Texas State University to become a social worker. Soon afterward I was hired at the Amarillo State Center for Human Development, a facility for mentally retarded individuals. What a joy it was during this time of interruption from my service as a missionary, to be involved in serving people who needed training and assistance right in their own community.

The Lord helped me to know more of His power and enabling through that position. Before long, I was asked to fill the position of director of volunteer services in which I was teaching volunteers, young and old, to work in the classrooms with the retarded.

If I had not stepped into the position as director of volunteer services, I would never have had some of the unique experiences with which the Lord blessed me. One of those was to extend an invitation to Roy Rogers and Dale Evans to visit our center while they were in Amarillo performing at a fair. They seemed happy to come to the center to appear on a local television program with our special children. My privilege was to tour them through our facility and spend some time visiting with them as we walked. I mentioned their little daughter Robin who was a special needs child and had passed away. It was during that time that Dale very clearly let me know of her born-again experience and how the Lord helped them walk through their times of grief. Roy and Dale had some foster children who also had met untimely deaths. They were prime examples of managing interruptions with moments of intercession as they walked the path of life. How I treasure those moments with them!

What I learned as a social worker and director of volunteer services enabled me to step out in faith a couple of years later to respond to the invitation to teach at the Arusha Bible School in Tanzania, East Africa. This would involve learning the language of Swahili when I was past thirty-five years of age.

Once again, the road ahead looked entirely too difficult, but I rose to the challenge as God enabled me. I fell in love with the people of East Africa, loved working with missionaries who were new acquaintances for me, and eagerly jumped into teaching courses assigned to me. Of course, Gwenda had adjustments to make as a young girl and pre-teen in new surroundings. She too felt the enabling of Almighty God, and He proved once again His faithfulness to us.

Actually, we should be thankful if we have a job a little harder than we like, for we learn a valuable lesson: *A razor cannot be sharpened on a piece of velvet!*

Throughout the moments of your day, lean on Him. Long for Him. Look to Him. Linger with Him as the answer for all you need. He will sharpen you, and your motivation will become one of depending on Him and anticipating His presence. Shake those feelings of inadequacy. Certainly, they are human ones, but God has better things for you. He wants you

God is eternal, without beginning and without ending. He knows all. He sees all. He needs you only as a yielded vessel through whom He can work as your enabler.

to enjoy being with your best friend, the Lord Jesus Christ. He wants to walk with you and extend to you His supernatural touch.

What a blessing you can know as he accompanies you on the journey of a lifetime. Believe for His enabling in whatever He calls you to do. You can be an intercessor for that one who needs your prayer at this very moment. Instead of saying, *"I can't do that,"* hear the Lord's encouragement in your heart, *"Yes, you can by traveling on your knees."*

SEEKING

Bowing low before Him,
I seek Him and implore
That He who is all-knowing
Would o'er my being pour

The essence of His beauty,
Tranquility and rest;
The glory of His presence;
His perfect will my quest.

Adoring Him, I linger;
Believing Him, I just
Confess my need before Him
And confidently trust.

—Sandra G. C. Drake

CHAPTER FOUR

Obeying

"Sometimes the people around you
Won't understand your journey.
They don't need to.
It is not for them."

—Anonymous

> ***"He said, 'You pray, I'll meet the need;***
> ***You call and I will hear.***
> ***Be concerned about lost souls,***
> ***Of those both far and near.'"***

I believe Frank Laubach had it right when he wrote, *"The trouble with nearly everybody who prays is that he says, 'Amen" and runs away before God has a chance to reply. Listening to God is far more important than giving Him our ideas."* In other words, praying involves our listening to God for the response He wants us to make.

With God's enabling comes our responsibility to obey. One dictionary defines obey, *"To follow the commands or guidance of; to conform or to comply with."* God calls us to follow the commands of His Word and the guidance of the Holy Spirit in our day-to-day walk with Him. Interceding in a moment of time calls for willing obedience.

Notice again the lines of the poem: *"You pray . . . You call. . .You be concerned about lost souls."* These commands were intended to bring the action of our obeying.

We may not understand the impressions God puts on our heart. He calls us, however, not to understand, but to be obedient at the moment He calls. Obedience is a major factor in intercessory prayer.

Why did 1 Samuel 15:22 ask, *"Has the Lord as great delight in burnt offerings and sacrifices as in obeying the voice of the Lord."* The answer may be found in the second half of the verse, *"To obey is better than sacrifice, and to heed than the fat of rams."* God asks for our obedience because He knows it is the better way of life. An obedient life is a peaceful life. Peace comes from knowing we have pleased the One who died for us.

The Message paraphrases Proverbs 3:5-6 this way: *"Trust God from the bottom of your heart; don't try to figure out everything on your own. Listen for God's voice in everything you do, everywhere you go; He's the one who will keep you on track."*

Many voices bid for our attention. We live in a noisy, clamorous world. Sometimes it is difficult to hear the voice of God amidst the cacophony of sounds around us.

A scene from West Africa is indelibly printed on my mind. Sheepherders brought their flocks to the Black Volta River to drink. Many different shepherds with many different flocks all mingled together. When the shepherds were ready to return to the home pasture and felt the sheep had refreshed themselves sufficiently, they would stand and give a certain call. With so many calling at once, the scene was sheer bedlam to me. However, amazingly, each sheep left the water and went to the shepherd whose voice it knew. Before long, every flock stood around its own shepherd, ready to be herded back home.

Oh, that we might respond so beautifully to the voice of our shepherd, that we might understand the importance of listening as a critical factor of intercessory prayer. Proverbs 1:33 points out, *"Whoever listens to me will dwell safely and will be secure, without fear of evil."* What a wonderful assurance

> Listen for God's voice in everything you do, everywhere you go; He's the one who will keep you on track.

of God's peacefulness. This comes only as we seek God in the closet of prayer or wherever we might be. Our responsibility is to position ourselves before Him to hear His inner promptings and to allow God's Word to instruct us.

The world that spins in turmoil around us is filled with people who would give anything to know this kind of tranquility. God has privileged us as His children to know His great strength in this way. How sad that we hesitate to take advantage of time available to spend with Him. The Word exhorts us, *"Be anxious for nothing, but in everything by prayer and supplication, with thanksgiving, let your requests be made known to God; and the peace of God which surpasses all understanding will guard your hearts and minds through Christ Jesus"* (Philippians 4:6, 7.

Life in a concentration camp and other devastating circumstances taught Corrie ten Boom that she could always enjoy inner peace. Living in obedience to her Heavenly Father, she learned to do what military personnel do at the end of long periods of intense, formal posture. They know the relief that comes when the commanding officer proclaims, *"At ease!"*

Corrie writes, *In the concentration camp, seven hundred of us lived in a room built for two hundred people. We were all dirty, nervous, and tense. One day a horrible fight broke out among the prisoners. Betsie (Corrie's sister) began to pray aloud. It was as if a storm laid down, until at last all was quiet. Then Betsie said, "Thank you, Father."* A tired, old woman was used by the Lord to save the situation for seven hundred fellow prisoners through her prayer.[3]

Betsie's prayer was indicative of the fact that she lived in a personal state of readiness to address God. She knew Him so intimately that He was her first thought in any moment of time. As Andrew Murray once wrote, *"God's listening to our voice depends upon our listening to His voice."*[4]

Corrie and Betsie had learned that no matter what life dished out to them, they could follow the admonition of Psalm 37:3, *"Trust in the Lord, and do good; dwell in the land, and feed on*

---

[3] *Prayer Powerpoints*, comp. by Randall D. Roth, Wheaton, ILL., Victor Books, 1995, p. 44.

[4] *Prayer Powerpoints*, p. 17.

His faithfulness." Feeding on God's faithfulness rather than on injustices and inequities causes one to center on how good God is. Forget resentments and grudges. Feed on His truth and love. Let His promises be your perpetual banquet. No wonder Corrie wrote concerning prayer that we should *"Quit struggling and start snuggling."* Keep close to Jesus and let Him nurture you.

In the midst of chaos and calamity, we can still take time to think on the goodness of God. If nothing else seems good to us at this precise moment, we must remember that He carries out His plans and purposes in our lives. No one can overrule His sovereignty. And that is very good.

Internalize the Lord's prayer as a continual model for desiring His will to be done on earth as it is in Heaven. For His is the kingdom and the power and the glory forever. Amen!

Verse 7 of Psalm 37 reminds us that we can *"Rest in the Lord and wait patiently for Him."* This too is God's call to obedience. We often feel that resting and waiting signify passivity and inactivity. However, the resting and waiting mentioned here speak of maintaining an inner posture of peace while going about our daily chores and obligations.

The soldier who stands at ease does not sink into a recliner. He does not let down his guard. He maintains his awareness of where he is, what is going on around him, and what the next command could hold. Although he is at ease, he maintains his soldier-like discipline. The soldier's discipline corresponds directly to the confidence he has in his commanding officer. Confidence, in turn, translates into obedience.

So it should be with the Christian, sometimes referred to as a soldier of the cross. Oswald Chambers once remarked, *"What an astonishment it will be to find, when the veil is lifted, the souls that have been reaped by you, simply because you had been in the habit of taking your orders from Jesus Christ.*

Everything we do as Christians is tied to obedience to God and His Word. Especially is this true in the area of intercessory prayer. When we truly intercede for another, we open ourselves to God's using us in some way to help meet that need. Praying does not get us off the hook, making us feel that when we have prayed, our responsibility is over. An intercessor keeps a song in the heart. The song might actually be a prayer. It might express the desire to be the hand of Jesus extended to the oppressed, touching Jesus and touching others that they, too, might be blessed.

Jesus remembered the thief at Calvary and ministered to him during the time of His own physical pain and inconvenience. How can we be any less open and selfless as we pray for God to use us in His service? Even during the time of interruptions in our own lives, we may have opportunities to help someone else. J. Robert Ashcroft, a great leader in the prayer movement, taught that Calvary is the other side of Gethemane. Prayer is not complete until obedience takes place. Jesus illustrated His Gethsemane prayer by His obedience on the cross. Because of one man's obedience, many have been brought into the righteousness of God.

How many times I remember praying for someone in sorrow or in the throes of illness when the Lord spoke to me during prayer that I should send a card, take a gift of food, or contribute in some way to help ease their pain. I wish that I could say that I have always obeyed those promptings, but I know I have not. When I have, however, I have felt the kind of fulfillment that comes only with obedience. At those times I have known the completeness of prayer and have heard Him speak to my heart, "At ease."

As we study the New Testament we see that prayer combines four important elements: (1) relationship to God; (2)

relationship to others; (3) action in response to God's instruction; (4) behavioral attitudes which reflect God's viewpoint in the matter at hand. First Timothy 2:1, 2 exemplifies these points. *"I exhort first of all that supplications, prayers, intercessions, and giving of thanks be made for all men, for kings and all who are in authority, that we may lead a quiet and peaceable life in all godliness and reverence."*

Out of Paul's relationship with Christ and love for his people, he prayed. He prayed for kings and those in authority, believing that as the people prayed, they would respond more submissively to those who ruled over them. In addition, the powers that be would make life easier for their subjects as a result of prayer. Prayer is seen to benefit those who pray as well as those who are prayed for.

Certainly, it is a win/win situation. Paul's example should teach us something very important. The daily paper and evening news can serve as wonderful prayer guides. Decisions made by government leaders may seem incredulous to us. We may feel saddened by inconsistencies and what we feel are broken promises. In the midst of each consternation, the Lord is calling us to pray. At that moment, we must plead for His mercy and grace, committing all things to God and asking His help in making us the kinds of citizens who truly bless our nation.

People in our lives with whom we have a difficult relationship or whose ways we cannot understand are people we should pray for. While praying, the Holy Spirit can bring us into obedience with biblical tolerance, godly compassion, and a greater desire for reconciliation with the parties involved. Even the people we have only read about or seen in the media that exhibit a lifestyle contrary to ours are people God has put before us to include in our prayers. It is easy to criticize, but it should be second nature for the Christian to pray.

I remember distinctly how the Lord spoke to my heart one day concerning this. As I drove down the street behind an old pickup truck, a bumper sticker on the back of the truck caught my gaze. It seemed I could not get away from the obscene message it carried. As I fussed and fumed to myself about the fact that I was a captive audience to something I didn't want to look at, the Lord began dealing with my heart. I looked at the man and woman in the cab, and I suddenly became aware that perhaps I would be the only person who might pray for that couple today. Who knows whether or not they would have another person call out to God in their behalf. I began praying for the Lord's intervention in their lives, and as I did, anger left my heart while a love for total strangers came in. In the following days, I often found my prayers drawn to that particular couple.

You might feel hurt, disappointed, and rejected by someone. Your mind becomes a whirlwind, and you inadvertently lash out with unkind expressions. Or you might be terribly hurt by a loved one's injury or illness. In the midst of all that, God calls you to prayer. Obey your Heavenly Father. Pour out your heart to Him. Unburden your heavy load. At the same time, listen to what He wants to say to you. Trust Him to guard you heart and mind like a soldier and to whisper words of peace from your commanding officer.

We pray. We call to God for help. We are responsible to be obedient. It is also our responsibility to remember that God is in charge. He asks for neither our approval nor permission. He promises to meet needs in His way and His timing.

> *The soldier's discipline corresponds directly to the confidence he has in his commanding officer. Confidence, in turn translates into obedience.*

As a child, my parents sometimes instructed me to do things that I did not want to do at the time. It wasn't that I wanted to be disobedient, but I had other plans and did not want them interrupting my schedule. I knew, however, that their directions were motivated by love and the best intentions for me. Because I loved them, I really wanted to please them. However, their demands did not always make sense to my young mind.

Sometimes I felt totally in the dark. but I learned early on that when I didn't obey, I suffered the consequences. They could demonstrate their displeasure in ways that very much disturbed me. Unquestionably, I fared best when choosing the path of obedience.

Abraham must have had similar feelings when God called him to leave his homeland and go to a strange place. I'm sure he experienced scary moments contemplating what might be ahead in that foreign country. He might have wished for different instructions. But Hebrews 11:8 records, *"By faith Abraham obeyed when he was called to go out to the place which he would receive as an inheritance. And he went out, now knowing where he was going."*

Abraham chose to walk by faith rather than sight. Because he chose the way of obedience, God blessed him and his descendants. God's promise was fulfilled as he was told. He obeyed the opportunity with which he was presented.

A poem written a long time ago by some anonymous author says, *"The stairs of opportunity are sometimes hard to climb; and that can only be well done by one step at a time. But he who would go to the top, ne'er sits down and despairs; instead of staring up the steps, he just steps up the stairs."*

God promises to be with us on the journey of a lifetime. His moment-by-moment promptings give instruction and direction. We, the pray-ers, are blessed with the peace of obedience.

Those we pray for are blessed with needs being met. One day, at the end of our journey, God will allow us to meet them. We'll be glad we answered the call to become concerned about *"those both far and near."*

For now though, we look forward to many more opportunities to follow God's instruction and be obedient in those moments of intercession. The time might be neither convenient nor comfortable, but we will obey the prompting of God. As Phillips Brooks said, *"Duty makes us do things well, but love makes us do them beautifully."*

According to God's Word, this is better than sacrifice!

COMMISSIONED

He did not ask for great renown
Nor seek for world-wide fame;
Men's applause He did not know,
But rather scorn and shame.

Yet this Christ gave all He had
That we might know His glory;
And now His call comes strong and clear,
"Go tell the world my story."

'Twas not God's plan that only we
Should hear and know His Word;
While there are souls around the globe
Who never once have heard.

He doesn't ask us all to go
To lands across the sea;
But, He does ask for yielded lives,
My friend, of you and me.

—Sandra G. C. Drake

CHAPTER FIVE

Submitting

**"To fulfill God's perfect design for you
requires your total surrender—
complete abandonment of yourself to Him."**

—Oswald Chambers

> *"And so I tried it; knelt in prayer,*
> *gave up some hours of ease.*
> *I felt the Lord right by my side*
> *while traveling on my knees."*

God forbid that we should present gifts to the Lord, but withhold ourselves. Samuel Chadwick exclaimed, *"Prayer is the acid test of devotion."*

Jesus is our greatest example of total submission. His prayer in the Garden of Gethsemane epitomizes His very reason for being. *"O My Father, if it is possible, let this cup pass from Me; nevertheless, not as I will, but as You will'* (Matthew 26:39).

The Son of God at that moment in Gethsemane lived as a human being with emotional and physical feelings akin to ours. "Drinking the cup" involved taking upon himself the sin He had never known. He became our substitute on the cross, dying in our place. I do not wonder that He prayed the same prayer three times before encountering His betrayer. While those closest to Him slept, He persisted in His commitment to do the Father's will.

Submitting means giving up control of self. Further, it is yielding oneself to the authority or will of another. Giving to the Lord those times that we could be indulging in our own pleasures or *"hours of ease,"* is an act of submission. Fasting our time and our food to be with God and His Word is a very spiritually satisfying exercise in submission. Another is the submission of our moments to the prompting of the Holy Spirit that we might pray for other people.

Paul reminds us in Philippians 2:21 that the world around us doesn't exhort us to submit to God. *"All seek their own, not the things which are of Christ Jesus."* In 1 Corinthians 10:24, Paul again teaches, *"Let no one seek his own, but each one the other's well-being."* Without submitting to God, we have no desire to submit to one another or to care for others' needs. When we draw back from God, we become very self-centered and greedy.

At age twenty-one, my first husband Sid and I planned our wedding around the theme of submission. In fact, that was the title of one of the songs sung.

The chorus spoke of not being what I wish to be and not going where I wish to go. But who am I that I should choose my own way? It's better far for me to let the Lord choose; to let Him determine whether I should go or stay.

These words clearly expressed our heart, for we had committed our lives to foreign missionary service. Together, we planned to follow Him wherever He would lead.

Later I learned that my second husband Myron and his first wife Marjorie had this sung at their wedding also. As laypeople, they determined that God would lead them in their service for Him.

What a beautiful picture of submitting to God! One couple who submitted to God's choice left home and went to Africa in God's perfect will. Another couple submitted to God's choice, stayed home, and served their local church in God's perfect will. One couple responded to God's call to "Go." The other couple responded to God's call to support in finance and prayer those who go. Both couples gave their lives to God, allowed Him to choose their path, and walked that path for His glory.

Both couples faced sadness in the years that followed, My husband Sid and Myron's wife Marjorie went unexpectedly to meet the Lord. Their deaths were years apart, but God's plan was being formed. Sid and Marge were first cousins, and their spouses, Myron and I, eventually found each other. We feel that having submitted our lives to the Lord for a lifetime, He led us to unite in marriage. We had a wonderful twenty-two years together before Myron passed away due to cancer. I faced another life interruption which you will read more about later.

The Lord deals with each of us on an individual basis. His call in Matthew 9:9 was, *"Follow Me."* Matthew, a tax collector, arose and followed Jesus. Details of how he followed Jesus were not given. Matthew, like all of us, was taught to love the Lord, submit to Him, and live life fully to please the Father.

The way you submit to God in prayer may be different from that of your dad, mother, or best friend. James 4:7 states simply, *"Submit to God."* Our task is to yield ourselves to the Master as we follow Him day by day.

Our hearts must be in a continual state of submission so we can respond to the Holy Spirit's prompting at any given moment. In other words, we each must keep our heart in a kneeling position.

Fasting is another form of submitting ourselves to God. When we would rather spend time feasting on His presence, we find it easy to forego our food, our fancies, and other forms of distraction. May God help us to develop more of a hunger for Him.*"That I might know Him and the power of His resurrection, and the fellowship of His sufferings, being conformed to His death,"* (Philippians 3:10).

The Psalmist knew about keeping his heart open to God's instructions, for he said on one occasion, *"I will bless the Lord who has given me counsel. My heart instructs me in the night seasons"* (Psalm 16:7). Even during those "moments of ease," his relationship with God was one of readiness to hear His voice. How special I feel when the Lord beckons me to spend time in prayer during the night when sleep evades me. I know that in the same way He can lay my need upon some sleepless one's heart. Not only is this reassuring, but it also elicits my faithfulness.

An Old Testament passage shows the elderly Eli telling Samuel, *"Go, lie down, and it shall be, if He calls you, that you must say, 'Speak, Lord, for Your servant hears'"* (1 Samuel 3:9).

God uses young and old alike who commit themselves to this kind of praying. He is no respecter of age, gender, or race. The ministry of intercessory prayer is the journey of a lifetime, available to all who submit themselves to the Lord.

Hours of ease quoted in the poem might consist of moments of leisure or self-satisfaction. Our world is becoming one of more and more leisure time. A more relaxed atmosphere has even found its way into the work place. We need only to look at the multiplied thousands attending sporting events each week to understand that people are looking for fun and relaxation. In the midst of all this, however, let's not forget that God waits for each moment we might give to Him, even a moment of ease. That may be the very moment someone waits for our intercessory prayer.

To be at our very best in using moments of prayer, we must stay alert to the many prayer guides around us. They may not be identified as prayer guides, but God can help us use them as such. For example, the church bulletin we receive each week can guide our hearts in prayer. Besides providing a calendar of events to pray for, the bulletin often lists the pastoral staff, Sunday School teachers and officers, church board, and other church personnel. Each leader in local church ministry needs the prayerful support of intercessors from the congregation.

I like to pray consistently for our home and foreign missionaries and their children. A great help in doing this is to have a published reminder of their birthdays. Sometimes I even put those in my personal organizer so I can have them available at home or away when I carry my notebook with me. This serves as a prayer guide and a tool for missions.

Many times I glance at my personal organizer, write a note or seek a date on the calendar, and some missionary or their children come to my mind. I can send a quick prayer for them to the throne of God. Although I don't count the minutes involved, I know that by the end of each day, I have had the privilege of interceding often for these choice servants of God.

Sometimes the Holy Spirit calls me aside to seek God further concerning a particular burden He impresses upon me. In this way, I partner with the missionary in all aspects of his life and work. Especially during those times of my illnesses with malaria and typhoid, I felt definite strength and God's touch as people prayed. My earlier experience during my Bible training taught me the importance of disciplined daily prayer of this kind. So, I know He can use my prayers to help others.

Intercessory prayer involves sensitivity to needs around us. It involves an awareness of what is going on in our world and a planning that sometimes calls for extra effort on our part. I'm glad God does not ask us to check our brains at the door when we engage in prayerful intercession. Rather, he expects us to be spiritually prepared. He calls on us to quiet ourselves before Him, give thought to what He wants to do, and anticipate how He might use us in the matter at hand.

I heard one pastor tell about having the names and pictures of his entire congregation entered into his laptop computer. He felt responsible to be involved in the daily lives of his flock through prayer, even when he traveled away from home. Seeing their pictures helped him stay on track with love, concern, and intercession on their behalf. Perhaps he felt what Samuel expressed in the Old Testament, *"Far be it from me that I should sin against the Lord in ceasing to pray for you; but I will teach you the good and the right way"* (1 Samuel 12:23).

The last time I heard from that pastor, he was working hard to keep up with the rapid growth of the congregation. God continues to bless him and those for whom he prays.

Marjorie Holmes states, *"It's so easy to promise to pray for people, or just plan to pray for people, and forget. So many afflictions, so many tragedies or desperate hopes that cry out for intercession. Only an instant of my time, only a few words, a thought—and who knows? It may be the only word of prayer that person will get."*[5]

Other prayer guides present opportunities for us to submit ourselves to the Lord for moments of intercession. Consider the local newspaper. The obituary column reveals family losses. The page of support groups helps us understand many needs in our community. News bulletins alert us to pray for actual or pending calamities. The sports section, social columns, and even the comic section can alert us to pray for athletes, school personnel, writers, and illustrators. This is especially true when we see the promotion of non-Christian values and lifestyles. Perhaps we need to pray for the newspaper editor and staff that God would impress them to promote His morality and righteousness. Whether they know it or not, the community around them needs us Christians. Without the prayers of God's people, Satan has a free rein.

> *Intercessory prayer is a matter of submission; yielding ourselves to God's control. Let Him nudge you during the moments of your day to pray for those He brings into your circle of awareness. Prayer guides are all around us.*

Have you ever thought of the television as a prayer guide? Have you ever gathered your family during

---

[5] *Prayer Powerpoints*, p. 26.

the evening newscast to pray for people and nations in turmoil? Or, perhaps an ominous weather bulletin has been issued, and you and your family agree in prayer for God's protection. As we surf the channels, we become aware of programs that are detrimental and robbing people of their moral underpinnings. We quickly move away from such programs, but they too can prompt us to pray for advertisers who give support, writers who script them, and those who take part in communicating the message being conveyed.

Many program guides surround us. In practical ways, they give us opportunities for intercessory prayer moments. They help us focus on *"whatever things are true, whatever things are noble, whatever things are just, whatever things are pure, whatever things are lovely, whatever things are of good report"* (Philippians 4:8).God knows we need these reminders to submit to His desires while relating to the world around us.

As I move about the community and the workplace at large, I have learned to carry with me a notepad and pen to write down needs that people express to me. In the course of a day, it is quite amazing to recount what I have heard from people whose paths I have crossed. Not only does this help me pray for others in the body of Christ, but it helps me pray evangelistically for those who exhibit a need of salvation.

If we are devoted to the cause of humanity, we shall sometimes be crushed and brokenhearted, for we shall sometimes meet more ingratitude from humans than we would from a dog; but if our motive is love for God and submission to Him, no ingratitude can hinder us from serving our fellow men and women.

We know that what we give is never lost; only what we selfishly keep impoverishes.

Andrew Murray once said, *"God seeks intercessors. God needs intercessors. God wonders why there are not more intercessors. Do not rest until God sees that you are one."*[6]

Try it. Get on your knees or pray with a kneeling attitude, whatever fits the occasion. Even if you give up an occasional fun time, you'll be richly rewarded with the Lord *"right by your side."*

Intercessory prayer is a matter of submission, yielding ourselves to God's control. Let Him nudge you during the moments of your day to pray for those He brings into your circle of awareness. Prayer guides are all around us. So are people in need.

---

[6] *Prayer Powerpoints,* p. 22.

LIFE'S PLAN

God's ways many times are so hard to accept
When things cross our paths which we do not expect.
We say we're God's children; our lives should be so
That whatever we do and wherever we go,
All things should run smoothly day in and day out,
For this is God's goodness which we talk about.

Then God has to show us as we go along
That sometimes the theme of our planning is wrong.
For He's the great potter, and we're merely clay,
Because He is Master, He will have His way.
It really is best that we fit into His mold;
Even though there may be disappointments untold;

And though at the moment we don't understand
Why life brings reverses to what we have planned,
Still there is comfort, assurance and joy
Knowing our place in the Master's employ.
Thus, we press onward with Faith as our guide,
Content in this knowledge, *"In Christ we abide."*

—Sandra G. C. Drake 1963

CHAPTER SIX

Investing

"Don't dig up in doubt
What you planted in faith."

—Elizabeth Elliot

> *"As I prayed on, I saw souls saved*
> *and twisted bodies healed,*
> *And saw God's workers' strength renewed*
> *While laboring on the field."*

In 2 Samuel 24:24-25, we find the story of King David who was commanded to build an altar to the Lord on the threshing floor of Araunah, the Jebusite. This was in response to the plague which had come upon the children of Israel and killed seventy-thousand people throughout the nation. When David explained to Araunah that he had come to buy his threshing floor upon which to build the altar, Araunah was willing to give the threshing floor to him to use as he wished. But King David insisted on buying it, for he refused to give to the Lord a gift which cost him nothing. So David paid him fifty pieces of silver for the threshing floor and the oxen. Then David built an altar, offered burnt offerings and peace offerings which resulted in answered prayer, and the plague was stopped.

Truly King David invested in the Kingdom of God according to godly principles. Yes, God has an economic system which is different from the world's system and which operates on different core beliefs. The world would think it foolish to give away a portion of their income. However, those with eternal perspective know that giving a portion of their income is a wise thing to do for they are helping to expand God's Kingdom and are laying up treasures in heaven.

Sowing and reaping are involved in the economy of God. People may sow in tears, but they shall reap in joy. Mark 10:29-30, *"Assuredly, I say to you, there is no one who has left house or brothers or sisters or father or mother or wife or children or lands, for my sake and the gospel's, who shall not receive a hundred-fold now in this time—houses and brothers and sisters*

and mothers and children and lands, with persecutions—and
in the age to come, eternal life."

God's economy involves a system of divine prosperity as
the widow of Zarephath learned. She invested the last meal
she had during the time of a great famine by offering it to
the prophet of God. This investment brought her enough food
to last until the famine was over. Again, the secret of divine
prosperity is investing in God's Kingdom.

This is the principle upon which our intercessory prayers
rest. We pray on to see souls saved, bodies healed, and laborers
strength renewed throughout the process. C. S. Lewis remarked,
*"If you live for the next world, you get this one in the deal; but if
you live only for this one, you lose them both."* What we invest
in God's service is very much worthwhile.

When economic woes increase, news headlines report tragic
losses for the nation and individual states. They also describe the
ruin of families, their dreams and hopes. We all too often hear
the hopeless declaration of victims as they recount years and
years of work invested in those things which are now destroyed.

Scripture is replete with admonitions to invest and prepare
for future days with all their unknown hazards. *"If anyone
does not provide for his own, and especially for those of
his household, he has denied the faith and is worse than an
unbeliever"* (1 Timothy 5:8).

*"Go to the ant, you sluggard! Consider her ways and be
wise. Which having no captain, Overseer or ruler, provides her
supplies in the summer and gathers her food in the harvest . . .
A little sleep, a little slumber, a little folding of the hands to
sleep—so shall your poverty come on you like a prowler, and
your need like an armed man"* (Proverbs 6:6-8; 10-11).

Investing, therefore, is a process of planning for
future benefit. This planning involves evaluating present

circumstances, contemplating future needs, and working toward set goals. Working through this entire process requires a certain amount of sacrifice as short-term gratification is replaced by long-term commitment. Such a commitment must be kept sharply in focus throughout the moments of each day.

At the age of sixteen, I began to understand the principle of investing. My mother had tried to enforce this principle throughout my childhood. Her words came ringing in my ears the night I responded to an invitation to give my life to God unreservedly. *"You get out of life just what you put into it."* After serving the Lord these many years, I would add, *"Experience has taught me that investing my best brings the best returns. He gives grace sufficient for the journey of a lifetime."*

Paul told Timothy virtually the same thing. When exhorting the young minister to live as a godly example of a true believer, Paul admonished him to care for the gift that was given to him by prophecy with the laying on of the elders' hands. In 1 Timothy 4:15, Paul spoke of these gifts as investments which would produce the returns of maturity in Timothy's life: *"Meditate on these things, give yourself entirely to them, that your progress may be evident to all."*

First Timothy 4:16 reads, *"Keep a critical eye both upon your own life and on the teaching you give, and if you continue to follow the line I have indicated you will not only save your own soul, but the souls of your hearers as well."*[7]

What an investment! When I give myself unreservedly to God, recognizing that He has gifted me for certain tasks, I reap personal returns, and those whom I touch realize returns of eternal dimension. Yes, we *must*, "pray on" for lost souls, the sick, and the disenfranchised of our world. God invested

---

[7] J. B. Phillips translation.

His only Son that we might invest in others day by day, hour by hour, and moment by moment."

General William Booth opened the first Salvation Army center in 1865 in an East London slum warehouse. He is credited with changing the history of Christianity as well as the history of social work. Today the Salvation Army operates programs in more than 100 countries to help people in need: homeless families, the unemployed, alcoholics, victims of domestic violence, prisoners and their families, disaster victims, the elderly, and the poor—regardless of race, creed, or natural origin. One man's vision led to an investment for eternity. Untold numbers of lives have been touched person by person and moment by moment.

Jesus instructs that we should not lay up treasures on earth where moth and rust corrupt and where thieves break through to steal. All our investments, wise or unwise, demonstrate priorities of our life accrued from education, experiences, and our own personal relationship with Christ. Faith in God's mercy, faithfulness, and omnipotence will hold us regardless of the gains or losses of our investments. But, thank God, He gives sufficient direction to invest wisely.

Intercessory prayer is such an investment. This investment, however, is not made in money markets or business deals. We invest time, concern, and physical energy in others when we pray for them, believing God for their needs as though they were our own and helping meet those needs whenever possible.

We may feel we have so little of God's gifts, so little of ourselves to give to others. We may *lament*, "I am only one person. What can God do with the little I have?" A better response would be, *"Now is the time. This is the place. I am the person."* Each of us must take responsibility to call out to God for one who hurts.

A Catholic nun felt directed of God to lift the poor and dying from the streets of Calcutta, India. Mother Teresa was only one person, but she was able to establish the Sisters of Charity to help her minister to the needy multitudes. Many people have read of her courageous and successful efforts to help people die with dignity rather than in a dirty, isolated hovel.

I had the privilege of visiting Mother Teresa in her home in Calcutta during the 1990s. Never shall I forget the impact of her presence as she came into the living room to address our small group. This little barefooted, plainly dressed lady had an aura about her which spoke loudly of her connection with the Lord Jesus Christ. Her demeanor was one of a servant rather than an outstanding celebrity which indeed she was. As she visited with us, her Sisters of Mercy were having their evening devotions in an adjoining area. We could not see them because of curtains which hung between the rooms, but what wonderful, inspirational worship sprang forth from those sisters. They sang *"Majesty, Worship His Majesty"* as well as other worshipful hymns in praise to God.

Mother Theresa said at one time, *"I am a little pencil in the hand of a writing God who is sending a love letter to the world."* As a pencil in the hand of a writing God, the love letter she delivered was not framed in beautiful garments, jewelry, and all the other things we might associate with impacting someone else. No, God's letter from her life was framed in love for those who were hurting and left to die on the streets of Calcutta.

Tony Compolo has told of a woman who wrote to Mother Teresa some years ago. The woman had gone through a divorce and felt alone. She wanted to do something to make a mark in the world. So, she wrote to ask if she could join the Sisters in India and participate in Mother Teresa's ministry. That woman waited months for an answer. Finally, she received a hand-addressed envelope with a note that read, *"Find your own Calcutta."*[8]

This might sound like a harsh response, but Mother Teresa wanted this woman to know that there are people all around us who need God's love. We do not have to seek out exotic places. Until we can love those nearby, we need not think we can love those far away. As you pass people on the street, hear of problems via radio or television, or encounter someone with an antagonistic attitude, make it a practice to pray right then and there. People around you might not know you are praying. You might continue your daily course of activities with eyes wide open, but in your heart you are kneeling and believing God for His answer.

Investing requires sacrifice. Whether we serve God at our home base or go at His bidding to lands far away, we must invest ourselves in the process. Often our personal praying concerns matters that please us. We pray as though God's whole concern centers on our happiness and pleasure. However, a diligent search of His Word reveals that His highest concern is that we know and trust Him. To please God should be our highest goal and the motivation for our greatest investment.

Think of how the giants of faith in Hebrews 11 invested themselves for God's cause. The list includes Abel, Enoch, Noah, Abraham, and Sarah, who all died in faith, not having received the promises. However, they saw them afar off and were assured of them. They invested themselves for God even though the promised return on their investment was not immediate.

Hebrews 11:33-35 lists others who *"through faith subdued kingdoms, worked righteousness, obtained promises, stopped the mouths of lions, quenched the violence of fire, escaped*

---

[8] *Prism* magazine, January/February 1998, p. 34.

the edge of the sword, out of weakness were made strong, became valiant in battle, turned to flight the armies of the aliens. Women received their dead raised to life again. Others were tortured, not accepting deliverance, that they might obtain a better resurrection."

These all paid a great price to serve God, but apparently they felt it was worth the investment. They knew resurrection would come. Nothing in this world could compare with the hope they held for eternity.

What does it cost us *to "see souls saved, twisted bodies healed, and God's workers' strength renewed while laboring on the field"* as the poem suggests. What does it cost to be a prayer partner with our pastor, a missionary, or Jesus Himself? We know the answer to this question, but we sometimes ignore it. The cost involves the investment of ourselves in prayer whether the situation is convenient or not. Paul spoke of it in 1 Thessalonians 5:17 as praying without ceasing, making our moments prayers of intercession.

Over fifty years ago I became aware of a little lady in Ghana who was known as Toothless Mary. Mary scrubbed floors for a living. With the money she earned, she saved only a small portion for her own needs. She gave the remainder of her wages to provide funds for those who felt called of God to attend a

> *The cost involves the investment of ourselves in prayer whether the situation is convenient or not.*

school of the Bible for ministerial training. I am sure that while she scrubbed, she prayed for those whose lives she was touching. On her knees, in her scrub closet of prayer, she sacrificially invested in those who had not the means to further their training. Thus, she sacrificially invested for the sake of God's kingdom.

Parents, likewise, sacrifice for their children. Because of love, we provide the best we can for them. Because of our Heavenly Father's love, He has provided the very best for His children. He sacrificed His only Son to invest in our salvation, and He continues to invest as He makes intercession for us. He asks that we take the returns of His investment and make them work for someone else's advantage.

Bill Gaither copyrighted a song in 1974 entitled, *"Joy Comes in the Morning."* He speaks of true joy as that found in giving what we cannot keep (our own special interest) to gain what we cannot lose (eternal rewards). That is exactly what intercessory prayer is all about.

It took time for me to realize that my husband's death in West Africa constituted an investment in young lives. This was not an investment of choice. Rather, it was thrust upon us. Years later, however, as I reflected on it I realized that God arranged it to be an investment for His glory in ways I could not have understood at the time.

About twelve years after Sid was buried in Ghana, my daughter and I flew from our assignment in Tanzania to attend the dedication of a library in his memory. The library was located at the Northern Ghana Bible School where Bible training was in progress. At the time, a District Council meeting was also in session.

After speaking in one of the services, I was shocked, but pleased, to hear a number of those pastors, evangelists, and church leaders relate their experiences as youngsters. Walking to and from school each day, they passed Sid's grave along the footpath. In the oral tradition of their families, they had heard over and over the story of the young missionary's accident and death. At different times, they each felt God's call to kneel there and dedicate their lives to the Lord Jesus Christ. As a result, they eventually went to the Bible training facility to prepare themselves for God's service.

What looked like a great tragedy and waste many years ago somehow proved to be a worthwhile investment for the kingdom of God. He has a beautiful way of transforming what the enemy means for harm into a victory for God's divine good. My prayer continues that many other youngsters will hear God's call as they walk that footpath in Ghana.

Time and time again God reminds us to invest in eternal values. Our families, schools, governments, and society in general are at stake. How clearly His Word portrays this in 2 Chronicles 7:14, *"If My people who are called by My name will humble themselves and pray and seek My face, and turn from their wicked ways, then I will hear from heaven and will forgive their sin and heal their land."*

God says, *"Invest your humility, prayer, and repentance, and I will respond with forgiveness and healing."* How our nation needs the people of God to cry out to Him. Government leaders may not understand their need for prayer, but God promises to respond to our investment. He states further, "Now my eyes will be open and My ears attentive to prayer made in this place" (2 Chronicles 7:15).

Thank God for those who lead the National Day of Prayer each May, the World Day of Prayer each March, and other prayer emphases which alert us to pray for the nation we live in. His eyes are open and His ears attentive to every detail of our lives. Let's make our moments count and see our nation blessed.

The history of the Church recounts many notable people who have

> *God says, "Invest your humility, prayers, and repentance, and I will respond with forgiveness and healing."*

invested wisely and generously for God's glory. I had been saved only a short time when Lillian Trasher spoke in my home church. She ran an orphanage in Egypt on very meager funds. How she challenged and impacted my life with faith-building stories of her investment in little children! Many of those children grew up to become people of God in positions that later blessed the Trasher Orphanage.

We all know people who have touched our lives who might not be written up in historical chronicles. Yet they serve God willingly and with great commitment. I think of the volunteers who served in the National Prayer Center which I was privileged to direct. Contributing their moments to intercede for others, this army of faithful workers accounted for a combined total of thousands of hours of prayer each year. Marriages reconciled, bodies healed, loved ones saved, and many delivered from substance abuse spurred them on to invest more prayerful moments when they might have felt inclined to quit.

Returns on investments rarely come instantaneously. Anyone whose focus is only on instant gratification will fail miserably in the investment process. This is true in the business world and also in the spiritual realm.

The journey of a lifetime is made up of investing each moment available to us as a powerful force for righteousness. Lives hang in the balance. Souls choose between heaven and hell. Workers in the harvest faint for lack of strength.

God calls you and me to invest those moments in behalf of others even when we have to look past our own hurts. He asks us simply to, *"Pray on."* Don't become weary in doing well, but believe Him for the reaping of everlasting returns as you *"Travel on your knees."*

INTERCESSOR

When weary in body and painfully sore;
When sure that I cannot endure anymore;
When sleepless and fretful I toss in the night;
When care becomes burden and nothing seems right;

'Tis then I look upward from my lonely place,
In search of life's meaning in all that I face.
Perhaps He is trying, as only He can,
To get my attention on Him and His plan.

To pray for those people, those sent in His name;
To pray for the many for whom Jesus came;
Remembering His Body so scattered and worn;
Remembering that they too great trials have borne.

And here at my midnight, God's voice seems to say,
"Somewhere in my harvest, your night is their day."
So rather than worry concerning my state,
Rather than dreading each hour so late,

I join with Christ's Body who faithfully give
Their time and their talent that others might live;
While through me the Spirit does earnestly lead,
With true intercession for those in their need.

His joy overflows me; His touch is so real;
His Body is strengthened; His peace I now feel.
Thus, I have learned that in spite of my pain,
A midnight appointment turns loss into gain.

—Sandra G. C. Drake

CHAPTER SEVEN

Traveling on

"You don't choose the day
You enter the world, and
You don't choose the day you leave.
It's what you do in between
That makes all the difference."

—Anita Septimus

> *"I said, 'Yes, Lord, I have a job,*
> *My desire Thy will to please;*
> *I can go and heed Thy call by*
> *Traveling on my knees.'"*

A Dutch proverb says, *"He who is outside his door already has the hardest part of his journey behind him."* Six chapters ago, we embarked on the journey of a lifetime with prayer as our lifestyle. This exciting and challenging journey mandates our interceding in prayer for others in moments available to us. We can be God's messengers, missionaries, and means of touching our world for Him by "Traveling on our knees."

We enjoy sightseeing, and no longer see people as trees walking. Rather, we see them as souls in need of God. We lift up our eyes and look beyond our own immediate circumstances. We capture every opportunity to call on God for someone else. As we move about our daily world, we maintain a kneeling attitude of heart, looking for momentary opportunities to bless another life.

God's enablement moves us along as we journey. Without Him, our efforts would be futile. We could do nothing. Our trip would be a short one, for our strength and faith soon would be exhausted.

As we travel, we are learning to obey, for to obey is better than sacrifice. All the gifts in the world that we might shower on another person would seem as nothing compared to the gift of prayer we give in obedience to God's prompting. When we fail to obey those promptings, we cheat someone out of a precious and godly touch.

In prayer, we submit our heart and mind to His, for we desire His plan and approval in all we do. As Jesus prayed in the garden, so we pray, *"Not as I will, but as You will"* (Matthew 26:39).

Knowing that our intercessory prayer moment by moment is a great investment, we believe God to change the lives and circumstances of those for whom we pray. Only eternity will reveal those returns on the investments we make for Him.

Motivated by anticipation of eternity, we keep on traveling in prayer. God's Word implores us to watch and pray, for we do not know the time of Christ's coming.

Some years ago, a songwriter wrote about traveling on, In a simple chorus, he declared his motivation for continuing to journey with God. Because he looked forward to his heavenly home so bright and fair, he felt constrained to travel on.

Doing God's will while looking for His coming endows us with incredible peace. When we realize we are doing what pleases Almighty God, assurance builds in our heart. Saying Yes to the Lord signifies our acceptance of the job He assigns us whether it is great or small. We travel with joy in the face of conflict and experience tranquility in the midst of turmoil.

Oswald Chambers remarks about our life's journey: *"Happiness depends on what happens; joy does not, and every time you pray, your horizon is altered. Faith never knows where it is being led. It knows and loves the one who is leading."* That's the beautiful thing about intercessory prayer. God leads us when and where

> *As we move about our daily world, we maintain a kneeling attitude of heart, looking for momentary opportunities to bless another life.*

He wants us to pray. He has an uncanny way of drawing our attention to a certain person or event with the distinct purpose of praying. The Holy Spirit simply warms our heart with His presence and guides us in mind and heart.

In Luke 24 we read the story of two who traveled on the road to Emmaus the day the women found Jesus' tomb empty. Jesus drew near to them as they journeyed and asked what they were talking about and why they seemed so sad. The two couldn't believe that this stranger had not heard the news which had been circulating far and wide that day. So they told Him the story of Jesus' death, burial, and resurrection.

When they constrained Him to abide at their house instead of traveling into the night, Jesus broke bread, blessed it, and gave it to them to eat. At that moment, their eyes were opened and they knew Him. Also at that moment, He vanished from their sight. In discussion about these unusual circumstances, they said to one another, *"Did not our heart burn within us while He talked with us on the road and while He opened the Scriptures to us?"* (Luke 24:32).

Many times, the best thing you can do with your moments is to be with Jesus. Walk with Him, Talk with Him. Enjoy His company as you journey. During the course of each day, allow a Scripture verse or inspirational thought to build in your mind. As you do, be prepared for His extra blessing.

Remember the biblical admonition, *"Blessed is the man who walks not in the counsel of the ungodly, nor stands in the path of sinners, nor sits in the seat of the scornful; But his delight is in the law of the Lord, and in His law, he meditates day and night"* (Psalm 1:1-2).

We in the western world are people of action. We are not good meditators. Walking around contemplating life's circumstances does not satisfy our need for accomplishment. In fact, we usually feel it equals idleness.

Sometimes, however, we would do well to meditate on what's happening around us and to consider everything in light of His Word. We might ask ourselves the ever-popular question,

"What would Jesus do in this situation?" Who knows, He might strangely warm our hearts with insight and a plan for action. That plan might involve our calling upon Him to bring about needed change.

Prior to the 1997 Promise Keepers gathering in Washington, D.C., men prayer-walked the meeting area and city streets. They walked singly, in pairs, and in groups, claiming the city for Christ. An executive director of the National Day of Prayer at that time reported that this "Sacred Assembly of Men" drew over 1.2 million men and had a dramatic life-changing impact on those who attended.

Similarly, several years ago when Focus on the Family held their "Renewing the Heart" conference in Nashville, Tennessee, forty men walked around the coliseum in prayer while women walked inside praying and believing that each seat occupied would bring that person to Christ. The conference planners expected 16,000 women, but over 19,000 attended with thousands more on a waiting list according to the newsletter of the National Day of Prayer.

God heard the prayers of those who walked and prayed in faith. Those traveling prayer warriors diligently sought God. Though their feet were moving, their hearts were kneeling before Him.

These illustrations took place some years ago, but today crowds are growing at special events for men, women, and children as a result of volunteer prayer teams who hold tight to God's hand and believe Him as they pray. Seeking God for Him to move throughout the nation and the world are certainly not efforts which are out-of-date. *"Jesus Christ is the same yesterday, today, and forever."*

Church members have been known to divide their cities into zones. Each zone has a leader, and the leaders meet weekly to pray. The people living within those zones pray for their community businesses, schools, etc. as they move about the city every day.

Some cities have initiated "Shield-a-Badge" prayer emphases. Participants get names and badge numbers of police and all first-responders to pray for them regularly. They communicate with these brave workers to let them know they are being prayed for and to ask for any special requests they might have. Testimonies abound as to the merit of such a plan. Christians become alert to send up prayers for every policeman and fireman they pass. Those first responders feel warmly supported by community members making a winning situation for all.

In meetings I have attended, I have heard prayer leaders tell of other ways to practice moments of intercession. Sometimes church members meet briefly at the church for a time of commissioning. Then they get into their cars with a prepared prayer sheet. Following a suggested route through their city or community, they stop in front of specific places and pray right there in their cars with their eyes wide open. They also drive through the residential area of each person in the car, claiming those streets for Christ and asking God to use the members in answering prayer. At the conclusion of this kind of prayer travel, they usually return to the church parking lot to pray for community outreach efforts.

You might find it difficult to think of prayer in these terms. Perhaps you feel it is not "spiritual" enough to pray in a drive-by mode. It's natural for us humans to look on the outward appearance. It is our omnipotent God who looks on the heart.

Wherever we are on the journey of life, He travels with us and blesses us with opportune moments to meet Him in prayer.

During my mission work in Tanzania, East Africa, I drove daily to and from the Bible training school in Arusha. The trip was a short one, only about 7.5 miles one way. Because of my teaching load and many activities at the school, however, I made the trip two or three times a day.

My heart became more and more burdened as I observed the throngs of Waarusha and Maasai tribesmen along the route. They were the nomadic people of East Africa and were seen virtually everywhere. As I drove, I prayed for God to move among those people. The more I prayed, the more I became convinced that God wanted these people to respond to the Gospel. I watched them herd their cattle, I saw their children, and I prayed for their families. For a time I thought the Lord was calling me to make a change of ministry and give full time to the Maasai.

But when typhoid fever struck me during my second term in Tanzania, I realized that such a change of ministry would be impossible. Eventually I had to return to the States for further medical help which included two surgeries. Thus, I never did get back to the Maasai people. How grateful I am that God helped me understand that my ministry at that time consisted of intercessory prayer during my daily commute.

The rest of the story is that other missionaries have gone to work among the Maasai and have reported God's moving in a special way. Many Maasai have found Him as Lord and Savior. I know that many, besides myself, were praying and believing God, but I thank Him for the confirmation that He heard my prayers too in my daily "traveling on."

How thrilled we are to hear praise reports of people

> *Prayer. It opens lives to His kingdom. It opens hearts to fulfillment with God's light, joy, and peace.*

who once were homebound, bedridden, and generally shut away from society. Their lives had come to a virtual standstill. They were over-whelmed by their physical and emotional limitations. Then, thank God, some faithful Christian touched the hem of His garment and release came. Those formerly incapacitated people once again travel the journey of life with renewed strength and vigor as a result of miraculous prayer.

Maybe you were one who traveled with them in prayer at a very crucial time. You might have focused a moment of intercession in their behalf. You may never meet them during this lifetime, but one day all things will be made known. What rejoicing you will have together.

Ministry possibilities are endless. Whether or not you ever stand behind a pulpit is incidental. The fact is that you stand between God and mankind with the key to victory in your hand. That key is known as prayer. It opens lives to His kingdom. It opens hearts to fulfillment with God's light, peace, and joy.

Keep traveling, child of God. Keep moving through life with a wonderful sense of His direction. Daily, hourly, and momentarily keep your heart open to His bidding. The writer expressed it in Isaiah 30:21, *"Your ears shall hear a word behind you, saying, 'This is the way, walk in it,' whenever you turn to the right hand or whenever you turn to the left."*

Knowing God's direction is not a spooky kind of experience. There is nothing mystical about serving God. He is very real and deals with us in very real ways. His Word gives us direction. His Holy Spirit impresses and prompts us at various times. During prayer and worship, His presence tenderizes our hearts. We become more alert to His desires. Truly, that is the purpose of prayer. We believe for answers to needs, but more importantly, we get ourselves in tune with His divine will. We learn that His ways are higher than ours.

The Bible likens the kingdom of heaven to a man traveling to a far country. You can read the story in Matthew 25:14-30. He called his servants and gave them his goods. One of the servants received five talents, another received two talents, and another one talent. The servant with five talents gained five talents more. The servant with two talents gained two talents more.

But the servant with one talent dug a hole and hid his talent in the ground. His reason was that the lord of the servants was a hard man, and the servant was afraid. So he kept his talent safe by hiding it in the ground. He thought his lord would be pleased that he knew right where it was. The lord of the servants had a glowing commendation for the five talents and the two talents gained. To each of those servants he *said, "Well done, good and faithful servant; you have been faithful over a few things. I will make you ruler over many things. Enter into the joy of the Lord"* (Matthew 25:23).

I am encouraged by the fact that the assignment to be faithful is one God knows we can handle. He doesn't expect more of us than we are able to produce. Each of us can be faithful *"over a few things."*

Notice, however, what the lord says to the servant who buried his one talent. *"You wicked and lazy servant . . . you ought to have deposited my money with the bankers, and at my coming I would have received back my own with interest. So take the talent from him and give it to him who has ten talents. For to everyone who has, more will be given, and he will have abundance; but from him who does not have, even what he has will be taken away. And cast the unprofitable servant into the outer darkness. There will be weeping and gnashing of teeth"* (Matthew 25:26-30).

Being faithful to use what God puts in our hands pleases Him and blesses others. We each have different talents for His kingdom. He never puts on us more than we can bear, and He never demands more than we are able to produce. He does, however, call us to consecrate to Him the moments of each day and fulfill the duties He assigns.

God calls you to be an intercessor. Whether or not anyone else calls you is immaterial. This is His command and your privilege in the body of Christ.

Traveling through life, even on our knees, does not mean we are free from interruptions. Some of them are quite insignificant while others make a major impact upon us.

Five years after my first book *Moments of Intercession* was published, life was interrupted with the passing of my husband Myron S. Clopine. After more than sixteen months battling cancer, he went Home to be with the Lord. At that time, I had retired from the National Prayer Center and was serving as a chaplain at Maranatha Village, a nursing home and retirement center in Springfield, Missouri. My life was blessed beyond measure with the privilege of being involved in the lives of those needing extra help and spiritual sustenance in their later years.

Interceding in behalf of people at Maranatha was my strength even in the *"valley of the shadow of death.""* Interceding for others brought God's distinctive touch and healing to my grief-laden moments. I really didn't recognize it was a God thing at the time. Looking back, I can see much more clearly what He was doing.

Of course, Myron's passing in 2004 was another major interruption for me. However, I recognize now how much more manageable life's interruptions have become through my prayer journey with the amazing God we serve. Childhood interruptions were many as my mother was very sick throughout most of my growing-up years. Many times plans for special school activities and other functions were interrupted because Mother needed my care. Fortunately, after receiving Christ's salvation at the age of sixteen, I found the joy of interceding in prayer for her, for our family, and for others as I sat quietly by her bedside.

Physical interruptions presented themselves throughout my service in Ghana and Tanzania. Malaria became an ongoing concern; then typhoid; an appendectomy in Kenya; a twelve-year-old daughter's broken arm after falling from a horse in Tanzania; and other physical issues as the years have passed. Through it all, the Lord has been faithful. He has been faithful to bless and use my daughter in service to Him, and to bless and use me in ministry. I had the privilege of serving as Nebraska Women's Ministries Director from 1983 to 1985 from which I was called to Springfield, Missouri to accept the position of National Women's Ministries Director for our fellowship. During the summer of 1994, I was asked to take on the responsibility of setting up a National Prayer Center. Once again, I transferred to a new area in our headquarters and enjoyed serving there until I retired in late November 1998.

Family interruptions involved the passing of my parents and in-laws, my daughter's departure from the states to serve in volunteer missions assignments overseas, her subsequent marriage to a wonderful Christian man, Bill Stewart, and their move to Alaska. Yet, those interruptions continue to emphasize to me the importance of standing in prayer at a moment's notice. After all, it's a win-win situation when the intercessor is encouraged in the process of lifting others' needs to God and those prayed for see His hand of victory extended to them. This is a pattern I have seen again and again in my retirement as I have served as chaplain in several different settings. The Lord's provision for me has been gracious and full.

The Lord truly blessed me in 2007 when He brought David B. Drake and me together in marriage. David had been a teacher and administrator at Central Bible College from which he retired after 42 years. He has been honored to be named a professor emeritus at Evangel University here in Springfield, MO. He had encountered interruptions also, including the passing of his parents, siblings, and his wife Elsie. Together, we pray for others, minister in church settings, do hospital visitation, and generally know the joy of being involved in the work of the Kingdom. As Bill and Gloria Gaither sing, "Through it all, I've learned to trust in Jesus; I've learned to trust in God."

A quotation by Winston Churchill is so true: *"Success is not final, failure is not fatal; it is the courage to continue that counts."* God bless you in your daily travels. I pray the Holy Spirit will integrate the message of this book into your very lifestyle. For that is what prayer is all about. Whether you kneel in your prayer closet or call on the Lord in an opportune moment, you will be a winner, and so will those for whom you pray.

Someone has said, *"Don't let the best you've done so far be the standard for the rest of your life."* Every day is a new day in Him. Give Him your moments, enjoy your new horizons, and keep your heart always in a kneeling position. This is your ticket to the journey of a lifetime, walking with Jesus all the way from earth to Heaven!

As years continue, I am sure there will be other interruptions of various kinds; maybe ministry, physical, family, etc. We have no way of knowing. However, one thing I know for certain is that God never changes, and He will be faithful as He always has been. He is the God of strength for today and bright HOPE for tomorrow!

By God's grace, mercy, and power, I will strive to manage life's interruptions with moments of intercession. I believe it works!

> *"Yes, Lord, I have a job.*
> *My desire Thy will to please.*
> *I can go and heed Thy call*
> *by traveling on my knees."*

THANK YOU

Thank you, Lord, for Christian friends,
For love expressed each day;
For kind concern, for interest shown
While traveling on life's way.

Life makes many strange demands,
And will 'til we reach heaven;
But how much more worthwhile it seems
With friends that You have given!

Calvary's love goes deeper far
Than merely verse we read;
For Calvary's love is seen and shared
With friends in word and deed.

So, thank you, Lord, for Christian friends,
For gifts, kind acts, and prayers;
And may the smile of Thy "Well done"
Eternally be theirs.

—Sandra G. C. Drake

THE AUTHOR'S
EPILOGUE

Years ago I developed a motto, *"Traveling in prayer; the journey of a lifetime."* I learned, however, that traveling alone presents many changes and challenges.

A reminder of the year 1999 stands out vividly in my mind. Just after I retired from serving in the National Prayer Center, I was asked to go to the interior of Papua New Guinea to speak for a large Women's Conference . Because of the costs involved in such a trip, my husband would not be going with me. This was an intimidating adventure for me because I had read about the head hunters and hostile tribes living there. However, I felt it was God's will that I go, even if I must go alone.

Some of my neighbors became concerned about my traveling alone to Brisbane, Australia, where I would connect with a missionary from Fiji before going on to Papua New Guinea. Those neighbors insisted that we gather together for prayer before my leaving. At that time, the Lord dropped Psalm 34:7 into my heart: *"You are my hiding place; You shall preserve me from trouble; You shall surround me with songs of deliverance. Selah."*

Wow! What a beautiful assurance of God's provision for my needs at that time. I can honestly say that all fear concerning that trip subsided, and I looked forward to ministry for the Lord in that place.

When I arrived in Brisbane to meet my friend, Betty Trask, I boarded a bus to head to the hotel we had booked. On the second stop in the airport terminal, Betty boarded the bus, and we were together for our hotel reservations and for the trip into

Papua New Guinea. Even after the government fell apart, and it appeared we would be stranded in a very precarious area of Papua New Guinea, God provided a miraculous way for us to complete ministry there and leave the country safely. The intercessory prayers of my neighbors held me close during that time.

Widowed the first time in Ghana, West Africa, I was twenty-six years old with a three-year-old child. Twenty years as a single parent taught me I could cope with the lonely twists and turns of life as Christ became my daily strength and guide.

Widowed again at the age of sixty-eight, I became acquainted with a new perspective on widowhood. Twenty-two years of marriage came to an end, and by then, step-children, grandchildren, and great-grandchildren dotted the landscape. As a senior citizen, I saw loneliness raise its ugly head once again.

I could understand the Psalmist's question in Psalm 10:1, *"Why, O Lord, do you stand afar off? Why do you hide yourself in times of trouble?"*

Of course, I know that God never hides himself. He has proved His loving care over and over again in my life. Often, I have to remind myself that every event of life serves to nurture the growth and depth of our character. More than anything else, the Lord wants us to deepen our relationships with Him. This can happen only as we maneuver through life's course of bumps and obstacles, keeping our heart in a kneeling position and open to His wise counsel.

I love the truth of Psalm 37:3: *"Trust in the Lord and do good; dwell in the land, and feed on His faithfulness."* We do have a choice in life. We can feed on, dwell in, and despair over life's unfortunate events, or we can choose to feed on, rehearse thoroughly, and encourage ourselves in the faithfulness of God.

Always He hears our prayers, touches our family, and meets our needs. I feel so unworthy of God's blessings throughout my lifetime. As David Drake and I minister during this late season of life, we continually thank God for the privileges He gives us day by day and moment by moment. We want to magnify Him on every occasion.

Yes, certainly, traveling with our Lord in prayer is the journey of a lifetime!

—Sandra G. C. Drake

TRIBUTE TO SIDNEY R. GOODWIN

May 6, 1936 — January 1, 1963

Sidney R. Goodwin, May 6, 1936 — January 1, 1963

Grave at Misiga, Bawku Area, Ghana

*Sid, Sandy, and Gwenda, before
sailing to Ghana, 1962*

Gwenda in Ghana, 1963

TRIBUTE TO SID

His purpose in life was made clear in his youth
when God asked him to carry the Gospel of Truth.
From the day that God's will was so strongly revealed,
this lad set his face toward the great mission field.

After years of hard study and much preparation,
Ghana, West Africa, was his destination.
His countenance shone and his heart beat with joy
when he sighted the land that he knew as a boy.

Many prayers, many dreams were about to transpire;
to work for God there was his only desire.
But God had a plan that was different, it seems;
a plan that was greater than all this lad's dreams.

His work only lasted a few weeks and lo,
he was called to that land where God's faithful ones go.
It may seem a great waste of youth's talent and zest;
we may wonder and question how this could be best.

But he didn't wonder; He knew no defeat.
How could youth be wasted when Christ He would meet!
He had done what he could to fulfill his life's call.
He had gone with the Gospel and given his all.

"Yet In all these things we are more than conquerors
through Him who loved us," Romans 8:37.

Sandra L. Goodwin – 1963

FAMILY MATTERS

Myron Clopine & Sandra Goodwin; married
8/7/82; Myron passed away 12/23/2004

Gwenda Goodwin Stewart, Bill Stewart, Alaska

David & Sandra Drake married
2/14/2007, Springfield, Missouri

A PERSONAL MOTIVE FOR VOLUNTEERING

I care enough to give myself
To things I feel worthwhile;
For life is richer, self more blest,
When giving with a smile.
Many things demand my time;
Commitments great abound;
Family, friends, and needs untold
Are always to be found.

But caring calls for action now
Before life's day is spent;
And somehow duties will get done
If that is my intent.
So, as for me, I'll share my time
With those whose needs are dear:
And reap the joys that come to all
Who gladly volunteer.

Written by Sandra Goodwin while serving as director of Volunteer Services in Amarillo for the Texas Dept. of Mental Health/Mental Retardation in 1968.

A PERSONAL PRAYER GUIDE

SUNDAY: Sunday School and Services of my church; Souls in need; Spiritual concerns of loved ones; Scrutiny of the Holy Spirit in my relationships and ministries for Christ.

MONDAY: Mission America; Multitudes in cities, towns, and rural areas; Multiculturalism; Military personnel; Missionaries; Ministering chaplains and church planters.

TUESDAY: Touching God for local, district, and national leadership as well as schools of higher learning; Taking time to pray and fast for revival across our nation.

WEDNESDAY: World missions; Workers and missionaries in foreign countries; Word-of-God training centers and overseas Bible Schools; Wounded and persecuted in the Church worldwide.

THURSDAY: Teachers, students, and parents; Needs in our public and private educational systems; Tensions concerning unrighteous curricula.

FRIDAY: Families of our area, including singles and the elderly; Fragmented people on the Fringes of society; Frivolous, antibiblical corruption of family and social values.

SATURDAY: Sensitivity to others inside and outside the Body of Christ; Salvation of neighbors and others I witness to; Spiritual preparation for tomorrow's participation in church.

—Sandra G. C. Drake

AN OUTLINE FOR PRAYER MINISTRY

"Traveling on My Knees; the Journey of a Lifetime"
2 Chronicles 7:14-16

I. A CALL (Invitation; Summons; Battle Cry) from your pastor, church leadership, and our Lord himself:
    A. To face the challenge;
    B. To make the choice;
    C. To accept the charge.

II. A COVENANT (Agreement; Pledge) with others in the Body of Christ:
    A. To act obediently;
    B. To trust implicitly;
    C. To believe expectantly.

III. A COMMITMENT (Responsibility) before the Lord and His Church:
    A. To spend time at the altar;
    B. To sense the needs of others;
    C. To see prayer as a lifestyle.

IV. A CONFIDENCE (Certainty; Trust) in:
    A. God's Word;
    B. God's Time;
    C. God's Place.

—Sandra G. C. Drake

KILIMANJARO COUNTRY

'Neath the shadow of the mountain
"Neath its lofty peaks of snow,
Lies a country, live a people,
Whom I've come to love and know.

'Tis a land of rustic beauty;
Far and wide has gone its fame.
People come from every nation
Viewing wilderness and game.

But to those of us who live here
'Neath the mountain's shining spell,
The attraction which is greatest
Is the people who here dwell.

We've a message for this people
As they work their crops each day;
As they labor 'neath life's burdens,
As they seek a better way.

See the multitudes at market
With the goods they've displayed there;
Hear them bargaining and shouting;
See the lonely beggar's stare.

What a joy to share the Gospel
Of good news and hope for all!
To see lives transformed because of love,
Responding to God's call.

'Neath the shadow of the mountain
'Neath its snowy caps of white;
Lies a country, live a people
Who are precious in God's sight.

Sandra L. Goodwin, Missionary to
Tanzania, East Africa, 1973

PRAYER RESOURCES

Blackaby, Henry T. and Claude V. King. *Experiencing God: Knowing & Doing The Will of God.* Nashville: Broadman, 1994.

Boa, Kenneth. *Face to Face.* Grand Rapids: Zondervan Publishing House, 1997.

Bounds, E.M. *Power Through Prayer.* Grand Rapids: Baker Book House, 1972.

Bounds, E.M. *Prayer for Revival:* Grand Rapids: Baker Book House, 1972.

Bounds, E.M. *A Treasury of Prayer:* Minneapolis: Bethany House, 1981.

Bright, Bill. *You Can Pray with Confidence.* Orlando: New Life Publiscations, 1971.

Bryant, David. *Concerts of Prayer.* Ventura, California: Regal Books, 1988.

Chambers, Oswald. *Prayer: A Holy Occupation:* Discovery House Publishers, 1993.

Christenson, Evelyn. *What Happens When Women Pray.* Wheaton, Ill: Victor Books, 1975.

Delffs, Dudley J. *A Repentant Heart.* Colorado Springs, Colo:NavPress, 1995.

Duewel, Wesley L. *Touch the World Through Prayer.* Grand Rapids: Zondervan Publishing House, 1986.

Eastman, Dick, and Jack W. Hayford. *Living and Praying in Jesus' Name.* Wheaton, ILL.:Tyndale House Publishers, 1988.

Floyd, Ronnie W. *The Power of Prayer and Fasting.* Nashville: Broadman & Holmann, 1997.

Foster, Richard J. *Prayer: Finding the Heart's True Home.* San Francisco: Harper Collins, 1991.

Guest, John. *Finding Deeper Intimacy with God: Only a Prayer Away.* Grand Rapids: Baker Book House, 1991.

Hendricks, Howard, and William. *As Iron Sharpens Iron.* Chicago: Moody Press, 1995.

Holmes, Marjorie. *I've Got to Talk to Somebody, God.* New York: Bamtam Books, 1969

Lauback, Frank C. *Prayer: The Mightiest Force in the World.* Grand Rapids:Fleming H. Revell, 1946.

Moody, Dwight L. *Prevailing Prayer.* Chicago: Moody Press, n.d.

Murray, Andrew. *With Christ in the School of Prayer.* Grand Rapids: Zondervan Publishing House, 1983.

Musgrove, Peggy. *Praying Always.* Springfield, Mo.: Gospel Publishing House, 1993.

National Day of Prayer Task Force. P.O. Box 15616, Colorado Springs, Colorado, 80935-5616.

Ogilvie, Lloyd John. *Conversation with God.* Eugene, Oreg.: Harvest House, 1993.

The One Year Book of Personal Prayer. Wheaton, Il.: Tyndale House, 1991.

Schaeffer, Edith. *The Life of Prayer.* Wheaton, Il.: Crossway Books, 1992.

Spurgeon, Charles. *The Power of Prayer in a Believer's Life. Edited by Robert Hall.* Lynnwood, Washington: Emerald Books, 1993.

Tozer, A. W. *The Pursuit of God.* Camp Hill, Pa.: Christian Publications, 1948.

106

Trask, Thomas E. and Wayde I. Goodall. *The Battle: Defeating the Enemies of Your Soul.* Grand Rapids: Zondervan Publishing House, 1997.

VanderGriend, Alvin J. with Edith Bjema. *The Praying Church Sourcebook.* 2d. ed. Grand Rapids: Church development Resources, 1997.

ABOUT THE AUTHOR

Sandra Drake is an ordained gospel minister who has served as a pastor's wife and a missionary to West and East Africa. She has served as a chaplain in a number of different venues in addition to being a director of Women's Ministries on a district and national level. In 1994 she was founding director of a National Prayer Center for her Fellowship. Drake has written numerous articles and has been a sought-after speaker for church and retreat settings.

She holds a B.A. in Bible from S.A.G.U. in Waxahachie, Texas, a B.S. in Sociology from West Texas A and M University, and an M.A. in Bible/Missions from the Assemblies of God Theological Seminary.

Presently, she resides in Springfield, Missouri with her husband David B. Drake, former administrator and professor at Central Bible College. Although retired, she continues to write and minister.

Visiting Mother Teresa's residence in 1991

Sandra Goodwin Clopine Drake, Author

10614281R00083

Made in the USA
San Bernardino, CA
30 November 2018